THE TRIVIA CHALLENGE

NORM CHANDLER FOX

WALLABY

A WALLABY BOOK
Published by Pocket Books
New York

Another *Original* publication of WALLABY BOOKS

A Wallaby Book published by
POCKET BOOKS, a division of Simon & Schuster, Inc.
1230 Avenue of the Americas, New York, N.Y. 10020

ISBN: 0-671-53224-3

First Wallaby Books printing September, 1984

10 9 8 7 6 5 4 3 2 1

WALLABY and colophon are registered trademarks
of Simon & Schuster, Inc.

Printed in the U.S.A.

For Loreen Arbus
Who conceived this book with me;
Whose ideas, generosity, and energy provided
    nourishment
    during its gestation; and
Who joyously shared in its rapid-fire birth . . .
    With eternal love from your best friend and
    soulmate,

                              N.C.F.

Acknowledgments

This book required a massive amount of research, and I was aided in that task by some very able Associate Researchers. A triple round of thanks goes to Robert Rodgers, Clyde Derrick, and Valerie Hoffman; a double round is in order for Jeanne Feder, Julie Resh, Dana Hood and Paul Morgan, and Dennis Gutierrez; and a hearty round of thanks goes to Nancy Fawcett, Art Goldsher, Kym Wells, Janet Brown, Michael Artenstein and Rebecca Bailin.

I also want to express my gratitude to my editor, Melissa Newman, and my friend Ira Ritter—both of whom were in my corner when I needed them. A special vote of appreciation is extended to Jack Artenstein whose enthusiasm and caring made the difference.

CONTENTS

INTRODUCTION

The Trivia Rush is on! Human beings of all shapes and sizes are mining reference books to tap those veins of factual nuggets used in the trivia games now being played throughout the land. People of all ages are frantically digging up gems of wisdom to entertain and enjoy, to flabbergast and flaunt. Children are trading facts with the same zeal formerly reserved for baseball cards. Executives and factory workers are breaking up the tedium of their jobs by playing "Did you know . . . ?"

Since the pursuit of trivia requires mental agility, stamina and persistence, you need to get in shape for it if you want to excel. Therefore, consider this book your trivia training manual!

The typical trivia book makes the assumption that the reader can assimilate facts and figures at mind-splitting speeds. While the material may be valuable, it's usually not possible, let alone fun, to learn. Who wants to inculcate new information by going through an encyclopedia of facts? Most of us don't have the patience or capacity and little is absorbed permanently.

What makes *The Trivia Challenge* fun and unique is that it is first a game and secondarily a resource book. The likelihood of recalling or learning facts is maximized within the relaxed, convivial setting of a game. It's a game that can be played alone (like Solitaire) or with other individuals or in teams. *The Trivia Challenge* is a book for boning up on trivia *and* it's a book that can be played. Here's a way to make every passing moment count!

Additionally, this game/book has a distinct advantage over the trivia board games because of its portability. You can play *The*

INTRODUCTION

Trivia Challenge anywhere, under any circumstances, with anyone —or by yourself. The more often you play, the more likely your scores will get higher. As you start accumulating more information, your self-confidence will increase for future matches of this—and other—trivia games.

The book is divided into sixteen categorical chapters, each chapter dealing with one specific subject: Animals and Plants; Sports; Television and Radio; Food and Wine; Space, Science and Technology; Religion; Movies; Business, Products and Money; Art and Architecture; Medicine and Health; Classical Music and Opera; Geography and Travel; History; Language and Literature; Theater and Dance; and Pop Music. The final chapter of the book, THE INQUISITION, contains questions on every subject in the book, and those who survive this 20th century Inquisition will learn what is their "Migh-T.I.Q"—or Trivia Intelligence Quotient for Champions.

Each chapter is a game unto itself—or you can accumulate scores for every chapter in the book. What's important is to have a good time as you're stretching and strengthening your mental muscles.

The game rules are coming up next. Sharpen your pencils and keep handy your scratch paper for answers. You've accepted the challenge . . . so, start flexing those mind muscles and go for the gold!

Rules of the Game

There are sixteen chapters with fifty questions on one subject in each chapter. All the chapters are divided into four sections, as follows: the first fifteen questions in each chapter are the easiest, the second fifteen are moderately difficult, and the last fifteen are more difficult. At the end of each chapter are five "Mindbenders"—bonus questions designed for brains that like to pump iron. On the page following the Mindbenders are the answers.

INTRODUCTION

One Person Playing the Trivia Challenge Game:

The player can elect to take either the easy, medium or hard questions in a category—or all of them. One point is awarded to correct answers on the easy set, two points for the medium set and three points for the hard set. After accumulating fifteen points, the player obtains the right to try for *bonus* points—by answering a Mindbender. Answering it correctly, the player gets a bonus of ten points; however, if the player misses it, s/he must subtract five points from the total score at that time.

The Challenger:

The Challenger Game version of *Trivia Challenge* is for people who want to gamble on themselves and increase their stakes. Here's where you can leave the sandlot and enter the major leagues. If the player wants to accelerate scoring potential, s/he can invoke The Challenger. This forces the player to answer five *consecutive* questions from the easy, moderate or difficult sets. If s/he's successful, the score for the total five questions in the set is doubled. If s/he is unable to answer five *consecutive* questions correctly, the player must forfeit five points. The single player should keep a record of both *individual game scores* and *the score for the total book of games*. Since the single player is challenging him/herself, the player will try to better the previous score on the next go-around.

To summarize: you can play a set (fifteen questions), a chapter (fifty questions) or a book (nine hundred questions). You can play with questions valued at one, two or three points each. Or, you can gamble on getting five in a row right and gaining ten, twenty or thirty points (double the value of five questions), but if you miss getting any of those five consecutive answers, you forfeit five points. At any time, as long as you have a minimum of fifteen points, you can try to answer one of the five Mindbender questions in each chapter. Give a right answer and you gain ten bonus points, while a wrong answer means you give up five points.

Two or More Players (Or Teams) Playing the Trivia Challenge Game:

For each of sixteen games (chapters), the players can select which set of questions (easy, medium or hard) they want to answer. Easy questions are valued at one point each, medium at two points and hard at three points. Each player (or team) *alternates* asking a question (whether the answer is right or wrong). Any player who accumulates fifteen points has the right to answer a Mindbender. A correct Mindbender answer brings a bonus of ten points, and a wrong answer will cause the player (or team) to lose five points.

The Challenger for Two or More Players (Or Teams):

When there is a *ten point spread* between the losers and winners, The Challenger can be utilized. Only the losing players can challenge the winning player or team, who then has the *option* of answering five *consecutive* questions correctly. If the winning player can do this, s/he gets the point value of the five questions plus a five-point bonus. If the winning individual or team fails at any one of these questions, the losing side gets a five-point bonus. If, when playing The Challenger portion of the game, the player(s) miss one of the required five *consecutive* questions, it immediately becomes the other player's(s') turn.

The player or team with the highest score in each chapter game wins that particular match. Naturally, it will become more exhilarating—and mind expanding—if you continue playing as many chapters as possible until closing the book on one player's or team's *accumulated* score. It might just happen that each player or team wins eight games apiece, which would mean that the highest score from the multicategory INQUISITION would decide the winner. And then, you start all over . . . because the more you play this book, the easier it gets to be a Winner!

ANIMALS AND PLANTS

Set I:

1. What insect is attracted—sometimes fatally—to sources of bright light?

   ?

2. Outside of zoos, what aquatic bird is never found naturally in the Northern Hemisphere?

   ?

3. Originating in the tropics, what purple vegetable-fruit is now readily available in the United States?

   ?

4. Name the process by which green plants use sunlight to manufacture their food supply.

   ?

5. What is the largest mammal on earth?

   ?

6. The failure of what crop caused the great famine in Ireland in the mid-nineteenth century?

   ?

7. What is the reason that hippos and elephants wallow in mud?

   ?

8. What colorless, inflammable oil comes from coniferous trees and is used in many paints and varnishes?

   ?

9. What rear-pouched marsupial is often thought of as a bear and spends most of its time in trees?

   ?

10. What species of tree is the tallest in the world?

    ?

11. What drug is found in the bark of several South American trees and is used to treat malaria?

    ?

12. Name the breed of dog used most frequently as a seeing-eye dog?

    ?

13. In which species of spider does the female often have a red hourglass-shaped figure on her body?

    ?

14. To what family of plants do peas, beans and lentils belong?

    ?

15. What's the most common method for determining the age of a tree?

    ?

Set II:

16. What small, agile mammal is known for its ability to fight the cobra snake—and win?

    ?

17. What fungus is instrumental in the process of producing beer and wine?

    ?

18. What were the first vertebrates to develop jaws?

    ?

19. What herbaceous perennial is used both as a vegetable and as a coffee flavoring or substitute?

    ?

20. While an octopus has eight tentacles, how many does a squid possess?

    ?

21. How many life stages does a butterfly have?

    ?

22. What species of fish migrates from the ocean to the river where it was hatched, when it is ready to spawn?

    ?

23. What is the name given to the gardening art of shaping trees or shrubs to resemble animals or geometric figures?

    ?

24. Which is the largest member of the cat family in the Western Hemisphere?

?

25. Although rice is usually thought of as the staple grain throughout China, what grain is actually the staple of the Peking area?

?

26. Because of its speedy reproductive cycle and space-saving size, what insect is often studied by geneticists?

?

27. Why do lemmings march suicidally to the sea?

?

28. What plant does molasses come from?

?

29. What's the collective name for the free-floating, living microscopic plant and animal organisms found in the sea, on lakes and large rivers?

?

30. What type of ant must enslave other ants to take care of its young and procure food?

?

Set III:

31. What species of bird, found on the Galapagos Islands, were most important to Darwin's theory of evolution?

?

32. To what order of mammals does the duck-bill platypus belong?

?

33. Besides trapping prey, what is the other major function of the spider's web?

?

34. Besides the apple, what fruit was traditionally identified as the one given to Adam by Eve?

?

35. Name the state of inactivity that allows an animal to live through intense heat or drought.

?

36. What sensory organ do some grasshoppers and crickets have on their legs?

?

37. According to popular legends, which plant emits a terrible maddening shriek when the plant is touched?

?

38. How long does it generally take a scorpion to become an adult?

?

39. What is the meaning of the name: aardvark?

?

40. What bird breeds in the Arctic and winters in the Antarctic?

?

41. What is the one trait for which the plant, Nepenthes, is best known?

?

42. Why are cicadas called seventeen-year locusts?

?

43. What is the name of the thickened spot on the snout of turtles and crocodiles that helps them get out of their eggs?

?

44. Regarding butterfly behavior, what is the meaning of the term, "mimicry?"

?

45. What makes the Mexican jumping bean jump?

?

Mindbenders:

46. What African animal belonging to the giraffe family was not known to zoologists until 1901?

?

47. Name the now-extinct bird that was originally called *Walghvogel*—the nauseous bird—because of its repulsive smell.

?

48. What Swedish naturalist was responsible for the "binomial" system of classifying animals with a generic and a specific name?

?

49. On what medium does the genus of pin mold called pilobolus grow?

?

50. What is the purpose of the Jacobson's organ in snakes and lizards?

?

Answers

Set I:

1. Moth. While the mechanism isn't fully understood, it seems that after the initial attraction to the light, the moth becomes dazed and comes too close.

2. Penguin. Some attempts have been made to "release" penguins in northern areas, but the birds appear to scatter and die.

3. Eggplant. It's a cultivated herb of the nightshade family.

4. Photosynthesis. Chlorophyll is responsible for capturing the sunlight in this process.

5. Whales. For example, the blue whale can grow to be 100 feet long and feed sometimes on giant squids, which themselves can be as long as 65 feet!

6. Potato. A fungus caused the crop failure which wiped out one million people and was indirectly responsible for the major immigration of the Irish into the United States.

7. Temperature control. The heat is unbearable for them since they have no internal regulation of their body temperature.

8. Turpentine. Today, it's being replaced in paints by plastics and acrylics.

9. Koala. The aborigine word *koala* means "no drink," since the animal never appears to drink very much.

10. Sequoia or redwood. It can grow to 300 feet and can live to be 1,000 years old—although the average age is between 400 and 800 years.

11. Quinine. Being toxic to all cells, a good dose of this alkaloid stops malaria from developing in the blood at an early stage.

12. German shepherd. Incidentally, Seeing-Eye is the name of an institute founded in 1929 for training "lead" dogs for the blind.

13. Black widow. Although the red configuration is common, she is sometimes entirely black.

14. Legumes. It's the second most important source of human food after grains.

15. Counting the rings. A ring appears for every year as a result of growth during the sun/rain period followed by the dormancy of the winter period.

Set II:

16. Mongoose. While this plucky little animal rarely gets bitten in the process, it is not immune to the cobra's venom.

17. Yeast. It yields alcohol by causing sugars to ferment.

18. Fish. This makes them important in terms of the evolution of man from his supposed origins in the sea.

19. Chicory. It can be boiled for eating, or dried, roasted and ground to drink in water or add to coffee.

20. Ten tentacles. All of them emerge from the squid's head.

21. Four. The stages consist of: egg, caterpillar, cocoon, adult.

22. Salmon. They've been known to fight incredible currents and hop waterfalls to return to the scene of their birth.

23. Topiary. Some of the finest examples of this art were found in Louis XIV's gardens of Versailles.

24. Jaguar. They can weigh up to 350 pounds.

25. Wheat. It was from this grain that the Chinese developed noodles.

26. Fruitfly. Having a reproductive cycle of ten to fifteen days, this prolific insect also has only four pairs of chromosomes per cell, making it an easy study.

27. Population control. Usually mountain dwellers, lemmings move toward rivers and finally the sea when they become too populous.

28. Sugarcane. Also known as treacle, this viscous blackfish fluid is produced in the latter stage of sugar refinement.

29. Plankton. The plants are called phytoplankton and are primarily algae; the animals are known as zooplankton.

30. Amazon ants. Although excellent fighters and strong enough to carry off slaves, these insects have neither the bodies nor programming to get food or care for their young.

Set III:

31. Finches. Darwin noticed variations between species of these birds, and there are fourteen species of the bird on these islands today.

32. Monotreme. Along with the Australian and the New Guinea anteaters, the platypus makes up this small order of egg-laying mammals.

33. Alerts the sense organs. The vibration of the web on the spider's legs lets it know that there is prey in the web.

34. Pomegranate. Due to its origins in the Garden of Eden, the

fruit has been revered and in the lore of dreams, the pomegranate bodes well for a love affair.

35. Estivation. It occurs in desert regions and the tropics.

36. Hearing organs. It consists of a chordotonal organ on the tibia of each leg.

37. Mandrake. The plant is closely associated with witchcraft and sorcery.

38. One year usually. As with spiders, it takes several molts before the scorpion reaches adulthood.

39. Earth pig. The name comes from the Afrikaans, who named the animal for its appearance and its habit of burrowing.

40. Arctic tern. This intrepid bird travels 11,000 miles.

41. It's carnivorous. Insects are attracted by its bright colors and are caught on its slippery interior surface where they decay and are absorbed.

42. It takes seventeen years until the species becomes adult.

43. Caruncle. Snakes and lizards have an egg tooth that's discarded often after birth.

44. Protective coloring. Some species of nontoxic butterfly acquire the coloring of toxic varieties for protection.

45. Larvae of a small butterfly. The insect lays its eggs in the fruit, and when they hatch, they become active.

Mindbenders:

46. Okapis. Prized by pygmy tribes and resembling the extinct short-necked giraffe, the animal is nocturnal and hard to observe.

47. Dodo. After Dutch sailors gave the bird that name, Portuguese sailors renamed it *dodou*—or simpleton—because it was awkward.

48. Carolus Linnaeus. He lived from 1707 until 1778.

49. Dung. This mold also has an explosive method of dispersing its spores for reproduction.

50. Detection of smells. Once part of the nose, it somehow evolved into a separate highly developed organ.

SPORTS

Set I:

1. What was the first U.S. city to host an Olympics?
   ?
2. Who won the single sculls rowing event in the 1920 Olympics?
   ?
3. Who was the first Commissioner of Football?
   ?
4. What football team's home field is Three Rivers Stadium?
   ?
5. What team won the first World Series?
   ?
6. What was the first professional sports team to fly?
   ?
7. What is the oldest trophy for which American athletes compete?
   ?
8. Who has won the most singles titles at Wimbledon?
   ?
9. What is the unofficial sport of China?
   ?
10. Who was the first man to swim the hundred meters in less than a minute?
    ?
11. Who was the first man to run the four-minute mile?
    ?

12. Which golfer has won the most Master's Tournaments?
?

13. Which of the two baseball leagues has won the most World Series?
?

14. What was the name of world-circumnavigator Robin Lee Graham's boat?
?

15. Where is the U.S. Grand Prix held?
?

Set II:

16. What U.S. General competed against Jim Thorpe in the pentathlon event of the 1912 Olympics?
?

17. Where was the first football stadium built?
?

18. In which sport would you find the Onion Patch National Team Series?
?

19. In what sport did Pete Gray overcome adversity to excel?
?

20. Who scored the longest field goal in basketball history?
?

21. What's the oldest stakes horse race still in existence?
?

22. Who is the only jockey to ride two Triple Crown winners?
?

23. In what sport would you compete for the Waterloo Cup?
?

24. In what city was the first U.S. automobile race held?
?

25. In what sport does Dave Christian excel?
?

26. What is the youngest of the Triple Crown races?
?

27. What baseball player was known as "Diamond Jim"?
?

28. Who was the first Mr. America?
?

29. Who was the last bare-knuckles heavyweight champion?

    ?

30. Where was the first balloon race held in the United States?

    ?

Set III:

31. Who was the youngest man to win the heavyweight championship in boxing?

    ?

32. Who is the only man to win the Grand Slam of Golf?

    ?

33. What famous baseball coach disciplined and suspended Babe Ruth?

    ?

34. Who has hit the most home runs in the World Series play?

    ?

35. What NBA team has had the longest winning streak?

    ?

36. In what sport do you use the term "buzzard"?

    ?

37. In what year did they hold the "unofficial" Olympics?

    ?

38. Who is the only man to have won the decathlon twice?

    ?

39. Although the Rose Bowl has been played continuously in Pasadena since 1916, there was one year when it was played in what city?

    ?

40. In a famous Olympics games, who was known as the "Buckeye Bullet"?

    ?

41. What organization awards the Heisman Trophy?

    ?

42. How many Olympic Gold Medals does Mark Spitz have?

    ?

43. What was the first team to use a rubber-covered football?

    ?

44. What was baseball player Bill Dahlen's claim to fame?

    ?

45. Who is the only man to play in both major league baseball and in the Super Bowl?

?

Mindbenders:

46. Who is the only player to make an unassisted triple play in the World Series?

?

47. What is the official sport of Maryland?

?

48. What sport was originally known as "sphairistike"?

?

49. What is the length of a "stade"?

?

50. When Hanni Wenzel won two gold medals in the 1980 Olympics, what national anthem did the band play?

?

Answers

Set I:

1. St. Louis. Because of the great travel expense, it was the worst-attended Olympic Games; it was 1904 and only eleven countries participated.

2. John Kelly. Although he's equally well known as the father of the late Princess Grace of Monaco, he was also the last American to win this event.

3. Jim Thorpe. It was in 1920, and the position was more of an honorary one in an attempt to improve the image of football.

4. Pittsburgh Steelers. It's because the stadium is built at a point where the Allegheny and the Monongahela rivers converge to form the Ohio River.

5. Boston Red Sox. In 1903, the Sox came from behind in what was then a nine-game series to take it 5–3 from the Pittsburgh Pirates.

6. New York Yankees. Individuals had flown before, but in 1946, the Yankees signed a contract with United Airlines for the season.

7. The Stanley Cup. It was first awarded in 1893 to amateur teams. Since 1926, it has only been awarded to teams in the National Hockey League.

8. Helen Wills Moody. She took it an amazing eight times, in 1927, 1928, 1929, 1930, 1932, 1935 and 1938.

9. Table Tennis. In 1971, the Chinese invited the first U.S. athletes to China since World War II to a table tennis tournament.

10. Johnny Weismuller. Considered to be the best swimmer in history, he swam in two Olympics and set 67 world and Olympic records in his lifetime.

11. Roger Bannister. He first did it in 1954. Today, most milers consistently run it in under four minutes.

12. Jack Nicklaus. He has won it five times, in 1963, 1965, 1966, 1972 and 1975.

13. American League. They have won forty-six World Series, compared to thirty-four times for the National League.

14. Dove. He was only sixteen years old when he began his solo around-the-world voyage in 1965.

15. Watkins Glen, New York. Actor Paul Newman has driven in this race several times.

Set II:

16. George S. Patton. Then a young lieutenant, Patton finished a respectable fifth behind Thorpe.

17. Cambridge, Massachusetts. It was built by Harvard University in 1903, and at that time, it was the largest reinforced steel building ever built.

18. Yachting. It is held in Hamilton, Bermuda—a place noted for its onions, and thus the name.

19. Baseball. In 1945, he became the first and only one-armed outfielder to play major-league ball with the St. Louis Browns.

20. Les Henson. The six-foot-six Virginia Tech forward shot the ball an amazing eighty-nine feet three inches on January 21, 1980.

21. St. Leger Race. This horse race has been run annually in England since 1776.

22. Eddie Arcaro. He rode Whirlaway to victory in 1941 and he rode Citation in 1948.

23. Dog racing. It was first run in 1836 and is the largest-attended dog racing event.

24. Chicago. It was in 1895 and was won by J. Frank Duryea at an average speed of seven and one half miles per hour.

25. Hockey. He was center for the U.S. Hockey team in 1980. His father played on the U.S. Gold Medal team in 1960.

26. Kentucky Derby. The granddaddy of them all, the Belmont Stakes, began in 1867; the Preakness was established in 1873; and the latest arrival was the Derby in 1875.

27. Jim Gentile. He was the first player ever to hit back-to-back grand slams in consecutive innings.

28. Bert Goodrich. He won the first contest, held in 1938.

29. John L. Sullivan. Unofficially, he may have been the first gloved champion when they became required in 1885.

30. Dayton, Ohio. This 1876 race was a disaster. Seventy-five percent of the balloons didn't last the first mile, and none came close to the destination of Chicago.

Set III:

31. Floyd Patterson. He was twenty-one in 1956, when he defeated Archie Moore who, at forty-two, was the oldest man to ever compete for the title.

32. Bobby Jones. In 1930, he took the British Open, the British Amateur, the U.S. Open, and the U.S. Amateur.

33. Miller Huggins. Despite the fact that he was only five-six and weighed 140 pounds, Huggins reprimanded the Babe on several occasions.

34. Mickey Mantle. He has a lifetime record of eighteen home runs during World Series play.

35. Los Angeles Lakers. They won thirty-three consecutive games in the 1971–1972 season.

36. Golf. It is the term used for an over-par hole by a pro.

37. 1906. After the 1904 Games, it was thought that the Olympics should be held more frequently—every two years. However, it proved too costly and the idea was abandoned.

38. Bob Mathias. Winning in 1948 and 1952, he was just seventeen when he won the first medal. He celebrated by shaving for the first time.

39. Durham, North Carolina. It was 1942 and just after

Pearl Harbor had been bombed. Public gatherings on the West Coast were curtailed, so the game was moved to Durham.

40. Jessie Owens. He took four gold medals in the 1936 Olympics, to the great embarrassment of Adolf Hitler—since the games were being hosted in Berlin.

41. New York's Downtown Athletic Club. It was awarded for the first time in 1935 to Jay Berwanger of the University of Chicago. The man for whom the award was named, John Heisman, is credited with legalizing the forward pass.

42. Nine. In addition to the record-breaking seven he won in 1972, Spitz had won two others in the 1968 Olympics.

43. Georgia Tech. It was used for the first time on October 13, 1951 when Georgia Tech beat Louisiana State 25–7.

44. First player to steal home in a World Series. He did this in 1905 for the New York Giants, playing against the Philadelphia Athletics.

45. Tom Brown. He played first base for Washington in 1963 and then played with Green Bay from 1964 to 1968. He played safety for Green Bay in the first two Super Bowls.

Mindbenders:

46. William Wambsgnass. This otherwise forgotten second baseman for the Cleveland Indians did it against the Brooklyn Dodgers in 1920.

47. Jousting. In 1962, Maryland was the first state to have an official sport. Joust matches are held annually in Baltimore each October.

48. Lawn tennis. It was the name given to it by Major Wingfield when he first introduced the sport in 1873.

49. Two hundred yards. It was the length of one circuit around the arena of the ancient Olympic Games. It was also the length of the first recorded Olympic victory.

50. "God Save The Queen." Wenzel is actually from Lichtenstein, which does not have a national anthem.

TELEVISION AND RADIO

Set I:

1. Fred Gwynne starred in what 1960's TV police series?
   ?
2. The series, "East Side, West Side," starred what famous actor?
   ?
3. Radio's popular detective show, "The Fat Man," was written by what well-known author?
   ?
4. What role did Jon Provost play on the TV series, "Lassie"?
   ?
5. What popular TV quiz show began on radio in 1949 and had the same emcee in its television version?
   ?
6. What role did Clarence Williams III play on the "Mod Squad"?
   ?
7. What were the call letters of the TV station where Mary Tyler Moore worked?
   ?
8. What was the name of Maude's first maid?
   ?
9. Name the musical group whose TV show was fashioned after *A Hard Day's Night* and *Help.*
   ?
10. In the TV series, "Adam-12," who played the role of Officer Jim Reed?
    ?

11. How many seasons did the crime drama, "Mannix," stay on the air?

?

12. What was the name of Kate Jackson's character in "Charlie's Angels"?

?

13. Who played Carlton the Doorman in the television comedy series, "Rhoda"?

?

14. In the popular radio series, Lamont Cranston was better known as what character?

?

15. What was Tony Baretta's pet cockatoo's name?

?

Set II:

16. For how many years did The Perry Como Show run on television?

?

17. Name the series starring David Niven, Gig Young and Charles Boyer.

?

18. In the popular radio show, "Life With Luigi," the central character of Luigi was played by what actor?

?

19. On the TV series, "Wanted: Dead or Alive," what was the occupation of Josh Randall?

?

20. What was the name of Danny Thomas's first daughter on "The Danny Thomas Show"?

?

21. Who was the host on "The Dating Game"?

?

22. What was the name of Shari Lewis's most famous puppet?

?

23. On the Steve Allen Show, who played the "Man on the Street"?

?

24. What television series revolved around a pair of look-alike cousins?

?

25. What famous television actor played the role of "Opie" on "The Andy Griffith Show"?

?

26. Name the hostess on National Public Radio's "All Things Considered."

?

27. What opera was written especially for television?

?

28. Although the "General Electric Theatre" had no host in its first year, for its second season which actor was hired as the host?

?

29. Name the title of the show on the radio anthology series, "Suspense," that became so popular that it was repeated annually.

?

30. Who introduced the segments on Disney's television series?

?

Set III:

31. What actress's voice was used for the talking car in "My Mother the Car"?

?

32. In what city does the daytime drama, "The Young and the Restless," take place?

?

33. The actor, John Hillerman, who plays "Higgins" on the "Magnum P.I." series, appeared on what other TV series?

?

34. In the TV series, "S.W.A.T.," what was Lt. Dan Harrelson's nickname?

?

35. Name the actress who played the housemaid on Jack Benny's long-running radio show?

?

36. What special group on a long-running TV series did the character of Steve McGarrett head?

?

37. What was the name of Dale Evans's horse in the TV series starring Dale and Roy Rogers?

?

38. Name Wally's high school on the show, "Leave It To Beaver."

?

39. What was the name of the show involving Gary Moore after his "Gary Moore Show" ended?

?

40. What was the theme song of the "Gene Autry Show"?

?

41. On the radio show, "Our Miss Brooks," which actor played Mr. Boynton, the biology teacher on whom Miss Brooks had a crush?

?

42. What was the name of the dog on "The Brady Bunch?"

?

43. Name the show that was the longest-running anthology in radio history.

?

44. What was the unique aspect of television's "Winky Dink" Show?

?

45. Comedians Bob and Ray spoofed which famous radio soap on their popular radio show?

?

Mindbenders:

46. Who played Gale Storm's sidekick on "Oh Susanna"?

?

47. What kind of a car did "The Saint" drive?

?

48. Name the comedy character played by Mervyn Bogue on radio's "Kay Kyser's Kollege of Musical Knowledge."

?

49. What was the hometown of Alan Alda's character, Hawkeye Pierce, on "M.A.S.H."?

?

50. In the "Adventures of Ozzie and Harriet" on radio, what two actors played the original roles of David and Ricky?

?

Answers

Set I:

1. "Car 54, Where Are You?" This 1960s comedy series was about a team of inept police officers who shared a patrol car. It also starred Charlotte Rae and Joe E. Ross.

2. George C. Scott. Both Scott and his co-star, Cicely Tyson, were relatively unknown when this series about a New York welfare agency aired in 1963.

3. Dashiell Hammett. The lead was played by J. Scott Smart, who was actually a very large man. Hammett created three of radio's leading detectives: The Fat Man, The Thin Man and Sam Spade.

4. Timmy. He was a runaway orphan brought in by Lassie to the Miller household. When they moved to the city, he stayed behind with the Martins.

5. "Beat The Clock." Bud Collyer was the host. The TV version aired in 1950 in prime time and also ran from 1957 to 1961 as a daytime show.

6. "Linc Hayes." The character was raised in Watts and arrested during the riots there before he began working for the police squad on the show.

7. WJM-TV. The station was in Minneapolis, where Mary Richards worked for news producer, Lou Grant.

8. "Florida." She was played by Esther Rolle, who left the show in 1974 to star in her own show, "Good Times."

9. The Monkees. The show aired from 1966 until 1968, featuring this Beatles-like American group.

10. Kent McCord. His partner, Officer Pete Malloy, was played by Martin Milner.

11. Eight years. It made its debut in September 1967 and was retired in August 1975. Gail Fisher played Mannix's secretary, Peggy.

12. Sabrina. The voice of Charlie on the show was John Forsythe, currently of "Dynasty" fame.

13. Lorenzo Music. Throughout the entire series, he was never seen on camera; the audience only heard his voice.

14. The Shadow. This wealthy, young man-about-town discovered how to cloud men's minds so they couldn't see him, allowing him to aid the forces of law and order. The character was most memorably played by Orson Welles.

15. Fred. Tony Baretta was played by Robert Blake.

Set II:

16. Fifteen years. Aired on both NBC and CBS, Como won four Emmys, had Frank Gallop as announcer and Goodman Ace as script supervisor. Como still does specials.

17. "The Rogues." Composed of an upper-class family of con men, these jet-set Robin Hoods had a home base in London. The show also starred Gladys Cooper and Robert Coote.

18. J. Carrol Naish. The show's popular running gag was Pasquale's fat daughter Rosa, who was always after "little Luigi." Naish was typecast for years in movies and TV as an Italian after this show.

19. Bounty hunter. The role of Josh was played by Steve McQueen.

TELEVISION AND RADIO

20. Terry. She was played by Sherry Jackson, who left the cast in 1958 and was replaced by Penney Parker.

21. Jim Lange. He hosted the original prime time show as well as the two syndicated versions.

22. Lambchop. Her other memorable characters were Hush Puppie and Charlie Horse.

23. Louis Nye. His sidekick was played by Tom Poston.

24. "The Patty Duke Show." She played both Patty, a gum-chewing teenager, and her cousin, Cathy, a Scottish intellectual. The cousins would switch personalities at critical moments.

25. Ron Howard. Much younger than the Howard we remember on "Happy Days," he played Andy Griffith's little son. Others on the show were Don Knotts and Jim Nabors.

26. Susan Stamberg. Taped in Washington, D.C., with feature stories from all over the world, the popular daily magazine show is co-hosted by Noah Adams.

27. *Amahl and the Night Visitors.* Gian Carlo Menotti's opera about shepherds welcoming the birth of Christ was written for NBC in 1951 and was shown at Christmas for many years to follow.

28. Ronald Reagan. The actor also starred in many of the episodes, and he and his wife, Nancy, subsequently labored in a G.E. commercial.

29. "Sorry, Wrong Number." Agnes Moorhead played a complaining invalid who overhears plans for a murder on the telephone. The twist ending is that she is the intended victim.

30. Tinkerbell. At the beginning of each weekly show, she would indicate if the segment was from Frontierland, Fantasyland, Tomorrowland or a True Life Adventure.

Set III:

31. Ann Sothern. Whenever Jerry Van Dyke would get behind the wheel of his 1928 Porter, he'd hear his mother's voice.

32. Genoa City, Wisconsin. Rival soap, "All My Children," takes place in Pine Valley, USA.

33. "Ellery Queen." Hillerman played the role of Simon Brimmer.

34. "Hondo." The lieutenant's role was played by Steve Forrest.

35. Butterfly McQueen. The NAACP appealed to Miss McQueen to leave the show because they thought the role was demeaning. She resisted, but finally relented and left. Eddie Anderson, who played "Rochester" on the show, liked working steadily on radio and never left the cast.

36. "Hawaii Five-O." The pivotal character of McGarrett was played by Jack Lord.

37. "Buttermilk." The dog on the show was named "Bullet" and the Jeep was dubbed "Nellybelle."

38. Mayfield. It has the same name as Beaver's town.

39. "I've Got a Secret." From 1952 until 1964, Moore was the show's moderator.

40. "Back in the Saddle Again." Autry co-wrote the song with Ray Whitley.

41. Jeff Chandler. He played this role before he went on to become a movie idol. Eve Arden played the lead, and Richard Crenna played Walter Denton.

42. Tiger. Besides this shaggy dog, the family consisted of a widow with three daughters who married an architect with three sons and a pet cat.

43. "First Nighter." Supposedly originating from "The Little

Theatre off Times Square," it presented original half-hour plays and ran for twenty-four years. It first came from Chicago and then from Los Angeles.

44. In-home participation. Jack Barry's 1953–57 children's TV show had a drawing as its Star—Winky Dink. It utilized a plastic home screen the kids hung over the TV set and used to "draw along" with crayons.

45. "Mary Noble, Backstage Wife." Their parody was called, "Mary Backstayge, Noble Wife." Bob Elliot and Ray Goulding have appeared as a team on radio and TV, and had a successful Broadway play.

Mindbenders:

46. Zasu Pitts. The title "Oh Susanna" was adopted when "The Gale Storm Show" was syndicated.

47. Volvo. Roger Moore, the show's star, drove a P 1800 Volvo.

48. "Ish Kabibble." The show used a musical quiz comedy format and included singer Ginny Simms and Harry Babbit.

49. Crabapple Core, Maine. Hawkeye did his residency in surgery in Boston.

50. Tommy Bernard and Henry Blair. The two started as the sons and were later replaced by the real things. The supporting cast included actresses Bea Benadaret and Lurene Tuttle along with singers, The King Sisters.

FOOD AND WINE

Set I:

1. What stew is associated with San Francisco?
   ?
2. In which of our nation's states did bourbon originate?
   ?
3. What is the traditional Jewish Sabbath bread called?
   ?
4. Name the classic French dessert that's made with pancakes.
   ?
5. What's referred to as a "bowl o' red" in Texas?
   ?
6. What's the most popular beverage in Japan?
   ?
7. What do you call the classic Chinese cooking pan?
   ?
8. What spirits are served in an "ice jacket" for special occasions?
   ?
9. Name the herb that's considered a staple of Italian cooking.
   ?
10. What highly prized fungus is harvested by pigs and dogs?
    ?
11. What fruit is ninety-one percent water?
    ?
12. What high-protein soy bean extract is an integral part of Asian cuisine?
    ?

13. Name the spirit that's made by fermenting and distilling fruit.
?

14. What vegetable is really a type of thistle?
?

15. Can you name the most famous cocktail in the world?
?

Set II:

16. What resembles a potato and is frequently used raw in Mexican cooking?
?

17. What New York Italian restaurant opened shortly after the turn of the century and went on to become an institution?
?

18. What was the favorite alcoholic drink of the American colonists?
?

19. What classic Spanish dish takes its name from the shallow open dish in which it is cooked?
?

20. What nut's name in Indian dialect means "hard to crack"?
?

21. Name the popular Japanese dish that the Japanese acquired from Portuguese traders.
?

22. What whiskey is made from barley?
?

23. The fresh leaves of what herb are called Cilantro?
?

24. Name the French wine that has a short period for drinking it at its best.
?

25. What fruit is indigenous to Persia?
?

26. What spice is found in a star-shaped pod?
?

27. Which company is the largest distiller of whiskey in Japan?
?

28. Can you name the New England dish that derives its name from the container in which it is cooked?

?

29. What Japanese vegetable is often used in place of turnips?

?

30. What spirit's name comes from the French word for "juniper"?

?

Set III:

31. Who invented vichysoisse?

?

32. What meat was traditionally taken on roundups by cowboys in the old west?

?

33. Name the Chinese Dynasty in which chopsticks were first introduced.

?

34. What phrase indicates that the payment of excise taxes may be postponed until this spirit is bottled?

?

35. What spice comes in the form of quills?

?

36. What is the cheese made in Switzerland that's green in color?

?

37. Name the vegetable that produces inedible leaves on stalks that are used as a fruit.

?

38. What after-dinner drink's name literally means "push down the coffee"?

?

39. Which berry is a cross between the raspberry and the blackberry?

?

40. What highly esteemed Japanese delicacy can be so dangerous that eating it is considered "playing Japanese roulette"?

?

41. Which grape is used to make a spicy white wine?

?

42. Which seasoning did the ancient Greeks call the "king of herbs?"

?

43. What seed of an annual gluten-free grass is eaten as a cereal grain?

?

44. Which French Bordeaux wine is famous not only for its wine, but also for its artistic labels?

?

45. What flavoring is derived from the pod of an orchid?

?

Mindbenders:

46. Which U.S. president banned all wines and spirits from the White House?

?

47. Who is credited with beginning the canned-food industry?

?

48. Name the fruit that's a hybrid of a grapefruit and a tangerine.

?

49. What are the shiny, smooth sugar balls used by confectioners called?

?

50. Which U.S. president got his nickname while working in a flour mill?

?

Answers

Set I:

1. Cioppino. Invented by Italian fishermen on the Pacific coast over 100 years ago, it contains shellfish, tomatoes, wine and fish.

2. Kentucky. Originating in the late eighteenth century in several of the state's counties, it was named after Bourbon County.

3. Challah. This braided bread is said to symbolize a ladder to heaven.

4. Crepes Suzette. When this dish is served at Antoine's in New Orleans, the restaurant's lights are dimmed.

5. Chili con carne. Texans have a perpetual debate over whether this spicy stew of meat, tomatoes, and onions should be served with or without beans.

6. Sake. Brewed from rice, it received its name from the city of Osaka which has traditionally made the best sake in Japan.

7. Wok. Called a "kuo" by the Chinese, its centuries-old design is ideal for evenly distributing heat.

8. Schnapps. This is the Northern European generic term for all clear, unaged spirits such as vodka, aquavit or gin.

9. Oregano. It's a member of the mint family and the leaves are usually used dried.

10. Truffles. This gourmet item grows deep beneath the earth.

11. Watermelon. An African vine of the cucumber family, it comes with both red and white flesh.

12. Tofu. It's a custardlike soybean cake that absorbs flavoring of other foods.

13. Brandy. It's derived from grape wine and often called the "soul of wine."

14. Artichoke. Originating in North Africa, it is the flower head of a perennial plant now cultivated throughout the world.

15. Martini. Although there are many theories about its invention, the most persistent is that a bartender named Martini Di Arma Di Taggia at New York's Knickerbocker Hotel invented it in 1910.

Set II:

16. Jicama. Peeled and often used in salads, this vegetable is very sweet to the taste.

17. Mamma Leone's. Opening in 1906 at the encouragement of Enrico Caruso, it started with 20 seats and grew to a 1,500 seat establishment serving over 6,000 dinners on a busy night.

18. Rum. When the British blockaded the supply from the West Indies, Irish and Scottish immigrants began making their own whiskey.

19. Paella. Although varying according to the region in which it's served, the classic Valencia version contains rice, saffron, sausage, poultry, seafood and spices.

20. Pecan. A tree belonging to the walnut family that was cultivated by George Washington, the hybridized version has a paper shell that can be opened with your fingers.

21. Tempura. The Portuguese taught the Japanese how to deep-fry batter-dipped fish and vegetables.

22. Scotch. Made from barley that's been dried over peat fires, the whiskey retains a trace of smokiness in its taste and smell.

23. Coriander. It's a member of the carrot family and an important ingredient in curries and Mexican food.

24. Beaujolais Nouveau. Often fermented for only four or five days, it's usually drunk from November 15 until the end of February each year.

25. Pomegranate. Among the most ancient of fruits, its seeds are used to make grenadine syrup.

26. Star anise. Native to China, this dried fruit from an evergreen tree has a flavor similar to licorice.

27. Suntory. Making whiskey for over half a century, it is one of the top five liquor companies in the world.

28. Chowder. Conceived by the wives of Brittany fishermen, they made fish stews with milk in large pots called *chaudières* —or cauldrons.

29. Daikon. It's a large white radish that's peeled, then cooked or grated raw.

30. Gin. The French word for juniper is *genièvre,* and the spirit derives its flavor primarily from the juniper berry.

Set III:

31. Louis Diat. Beginning his career in Vichy, he created the soup while head chef of New York's Ritz-Carlton Hotel remembering his mother's potato soup which he enjoyed as a cold snack.

32. Beef jerky. The cowboys were taught by the Indians how to preserve the beef by drying it in the sun.

33. Shang Dynasty. During this time, from 1766–1123 B.C., chopsticks were made of agate, jade, silver and ivory.

34. Bottled in bond. This indicates that the bourbon is from a single distillery, made in a single season, kept in wood at least four years, stored in a "bonded" warehouse, and bottled at one hundred proof.

35. Cinammon. The quills are removed from the aromatic bark of a laurel tree found in Sri Lanka.

36. Sapsago. The color comes from the addition of clover to the curd.

37. Rhubarb. It's a member of the buckwheat plant family that originated in Tibet.

38. Pousse-cafe. The drink is composed of different colored liqueurs that are poured in layers in a narrow glass, and it's sometimes known as a "Judy Garland" because of its rainbow effect.

39. Loganberry. It was discovered by Judge J.H. Logan in 1881.

40. Fugu. This Japanese blowfish has highly poisonous testicles that can contaminate the entire fish if not removed carefully.

41. Gewurtztraminer. The best wines of this type come from the Alsace region on the Rhine.

42. Basil. Valuing its aroma so highly, the ancient Greeks used it in their perfumes as well as their cooking.

43. Millet. Grown throughout Europe and Asia, it's a source of starch in the U.S.S.R.

44. Mouton-Rothschild. Some of their labels have been designed by Chagall, Picasso and Andy Warhol.

45. Vanilla. Coming from a climbing orchid native to Central America, the beans are soaked in grain alcohol to produce vanilla extract.

Mindbenders:

46. Rutherford B. Hayes. Serving in office from 1877 until 1881, he never realized his wife was known as "Lemonade Lucy." Ironically, the Hayeses never knew that a steward would spike their guests' punch.

47. Nicolas Appert. This French inventor devised a means to preserve food in 1795 in response to Napoleon's offering a prize to anyone who could better feed his armies.

48. Ugli fruit. Developed in Jamaica, it looks like a bumpy grapefruit and is much sweeter in taste.

49. Dragées. The name comes from the French for "sugar plum."

50. Abraham Lincoln. While working in a flour mill as a youth, Abe was very honest in not mixing unnatural ingredients—such as chalk—into the flour, which was a common practice at that time. He became known as "Honest Abe."

SPACE, SCIENCE AND TECHNOLOGY

Set I:

1. What was the name of the command module on the Apollo 10 mission?

   ?

2. What is deoxyribonucleic acid more commonly called?

   ?

3. Name the synthetic fiber developed by DuPont that was rationed during World War II.

   ?

4. What is the particle of an atom that has no electrical charge?

   ?

5. What was the landing site for the Apollo 11 mission?

   ?

6. According to ancient belief, the four essential elements were earth, fire, air, and what was the fourth?

   ?

7. The sum of the interior angles of a triangle is how much?

   ?

8. Any material through which an electric current or heat can flow is known by what name?

   ?

9. Where do the droplets of moisture on the outside of a glass of iced tea come from?

   ?

10. What was the name of the lunar module on the Apollo 11 mission?

    ?

11. Which astronomer first insisted that the sun stood still and the earth moved around it?

?

12. What isotope is most frequently considered in the dating of archaelogical specimens?

?

13. What is the last of the planets visible to the unaided eye?

?

14. Who was the first American in space?

?

15. What travels at 186,284 miles per second?

?

Set II:

16. Who is considered the father of modern rocketry?

?

17. What was the first successful satellite?

?

18. What is the outer color of a common rainbow?

?

19. Who discovered that adding certain things to sticky, untreated rubber would make it stable?

?

20. After witnessing what event did J. Robert Oppenheimer think of the quote, "The radiance of a thousand suns, I am become death, The Shatterer of Worlds"?

?

21. In chemistry, what is the opposite of reduction?

?

22. What has a diameter of 120,000 light years?

?

23. In January of 1986, the planet Uranus will receive a fly-by encounter with what spacecraft?

?

24. Who coined the term "laser"?

?

25. Name the instrument that tests for radioactivity?

?

26. Who decoded the hieroglyphics of the Rosetta Stone?

?

27. Can you name the item invented by Whitcomb Judson that is particularly essential to men's clothing?

?

28. Which Apollo mission aborted in mid-flight?

?

29. Who built the first digital computer?

?

30. Recrystallized limestone is known by what more glamorous name?

?

Set III:

31. What National Aeronautics and Space Administration project landed a spacecraft on the surface of Mars?

?

32. If you were to fire a long-range cannon without considering the Coriolis force, in which direction from the target would your shot fall?

?

33. An armillary sphere was central to what profession?

?

34. Saponification results in what common everyday product?

?

35. What was the name of the lunar module on the Apollo 9 mission?

?

36. The assembly line process, which was utilized so well by Henry Ford, was actually pioneered by whom?

?

37. The eighteenth-century chemist John Priestley created the name for what product that originally comes from trees?

?

38. What were Margaret Mead's first observations into human behavior?

?

39. The Pascal Triangle is the basis for what applied science?

?

40. Why does coral grow close to the surface of the ocean?

?

41. Who was the first man to split the atom?

?

42. What was the first spacecraft to encounter Jupiter?

?

43. Of the seven orignal Mercury astronauts, who was the oldest?

?

44. In what country is the largest reflector telescope in the world?

?

45. Who was the first to fly the X-15?

?

Mindbenders:

46. Which Apollo mission spent the longest time on the surface of the moon?

?

47. Who invented the traffic light?

?

48. Who stated the guiding motto of the scientist as: "Seek simplicity and distrust it"?

?

49. Who set the record for the longest hot-air balloon ride in history?

?

50. Who was the first man to "walk in space"?

?

Answers

Set I:

1. Charlie Brown. Apollo 10's crew members were: Thomas Stafford, Eugene Cernan and John Young.

2. DNA. It contains all the genetic codes in animals and humans.

3. Nylon. This synthetic polymide was developed by chemist Wallace Carothers in 1935.

4. Neutron. The positively charged atomic particle is called a proton.

5. Sea of Tranquility. The commander of Apollo 11 and the first human being on the surface of the moon was Neil Armstrong.

6. Water. The ancients believed these four elements to be the building blocks of nature.

7. One hundred eighty degrees. This never changes. The study of triangles on the surface of a sphere, incidentally, is important in surveying, navigation and astronomy.

8. Conductor. All metals are good conductors of heat and electricity.

9. Air. Moisture from the atmosphere condenses on an icy surface.

10. *Eagle.* "The *Eagle* has landed" became a cause for celebration. The command module was named *Columbia.*

11. Copernicus. The sixteenth-century Polish astronomer was said to have uttered the invocation, "Sun, stand thou

still!" His system explained retrograde motion in a natural way.

12. Carbon 14. As a heavy isotope of the element, its rate of decay can be accurately measured and, in turn, can help date a given sample of material.

13. Saturn. Second in size to Jupiter, the planet's ring systems were shown to be more complex than realized by Voyagers I and II.

14. Alan Shepard. Commanding the Mercury 3, he was launched May 5, 1961, and the flight's duration was fifteen minutes.

15. Light. Scientists Michelson and Morley were the first to measure the speed of light.

Set II:

16. Robert H. Goddard. Having built and fired the first liquid-fueled rocket in 1926, he also designed the first practical automatic steering device for rockets.

17. Sputnik 1. Launched October 4, 1957, it stayed in orbit for ninety-two days.

18. Red. The inside color is blue or violet. If there's a second rainbow beyond the primary one, its colors will be reversed.

19. Charles Goodyear. He accidentally found that adding sulphur and heat made a versatile, marketable commodity. The process is called vulcanization.

20. Watching the first atomic bomb explode in the desert. His associate, Ken Bainbridge, just said, "Now we're all sons of bitches."

21. Oxidation. Usually the reduction of a substance is any reaction in which that substance gains electrons.

22. Milky Way Galaxy. A light year—the distance traveled at the speed of light in one year—is approximately 5,880,000,000,000 miles.

23. Voyager 2. The craft was launched August 20, 1977.

24. R. Gordon Gould. Having invented the laser, he chose to call it by an acronym standing for: *l*ight *a*mplification by *s*timulated *e*mission of *r*adiation.

25. Geiger counter. It also measures the strength of alpha, beta and gamma rays.

26. Jean François Champollion. An outstanding linguist, he had mastered the languages of Latin, Greek and Hebrew at the age of eleven.

27. Zipper. Judson called his invention the "clasp locker and unlocker."

28. Apollo 13. The service module oxygen tank ruptured, and the lunar module oxygen and power were used until just before re-entry.

29. Harvard University. It was completed in 1944 with a five-million-dollar grant from I.B.M.

30. Marble. It occurs in various colors, but the pure form is much prized for architecture and sculpture.

Set III:

31. Viking 1 and 2. Launched in August and September, 1975, the probes landed in 1976 and returned the first television pictures from the Martian surface.

32. To the right. The Coriolis force is an apparent force that, as a result of the earth's rotation, deflects moving objects to the right in the Northern Hemisphere and to the left in the Southern Hemisphere.

33. Astronomy. It's that handsome spherelike object made of several rings around a central axis, whose original purpose was to determine the altitude of celestial bodies.

34. Soap. It's the changing of fat into soap through a reaction with an alkali.

35. Spider. This was the first manned flight of the lunar module.

36. Eli Whitney. He developed it while fulfilling a government contract for muskets in 1798.

37. Rubber. Priestley's fame, however, came from his discovery of oxygen in 1774.

38. Speech patterns. She spent much time recording the speech configurations of her younger sister.

39. Statistics. The Pascal Triangle is used to show probability theory in a graphic form.

40. It needs sunlight. The colonies of tiny animals gradually build up reefs, which cause dangerous subsurface hazards to navigation.

41. Ernest Rutherford. The English scientist also discovered and named alpha and beta radiation. He's called the father of nuclear physics.

42. Pioneer 10. The probe encountered the largest planet on December 3, 1973.

43. John Glenn. Glenn, at thirty-seven, had a few more years over Deke Slayton, thirty-five, Scott Carpenter, thirty-four and Gus Grissom, thirty-three.

44. U.S.S.R. It's the 236-inch mirror at the Special Astrophysical Observatory in the Caucasus of the Soviet Union. The next largest is the 200-inch reflector at California's Mount Palomar Observatory.

45. Scott Crossfield. He was a contract pilot for North American Aviation. Chuck Yeager, on the other hand, was the first man to break the sound barrier in flight.

Mindbenders:

46. Apollo 17. Eugene Cernan and Harrison Schmitt spent a record seventy-five hours on the moon. The total duration of the mission was 301 hours.

47. William M. Potts. He was a Detroit policeman.

48. Alfred North Whitehead. The English mathematician and and philosopher who taught at Harvard, warned that we are apt to fall into the error of thinking that the facts are simple because simplicity is the goal of our quest.

49. Ben Abruzzo and Maxie Anderson. The flew from Presque Isle, Maine to Miserey, France for a duration of 137 hours, 5 minutes and 50 soconds in August, 1978.

50. Aleksei Leonov. His ten-minute "space walk" in March 1965 made history. The first American to walk in space was Edward White, who made a twenty-minute stroll in June 1965.

RELIGION

Set I:

1. Who founded the Dominican Order of Monks?
   ?
2. What ancient philosopher influenced St. Thomas Aquinas?
   ?
3. In what country is Ephesus?
   ?
4. Who directed the film *The Bible*?
   ?
5. What's the symbol on the Pope's ring?
   ?
6. What did the Lord send to Moses and his people to eat when they ran out of food in Sinai?
   ?
7. In the Islamic religion, who is El Kahil?
   ?
8. Who was the first Apostle to whom Jesus appeared?
   ?
9. Name the Greek god whose wine festivals brought about the earliest forms of theater.
   ?
10. Gautama Siddhartha was the founder of what eastern religion?
    ?
11. Martin Luther was a native of what country?
    ?
12. Which is the "earliest and briefest" of the Gospels?
    ?

13. Who was the mother of John the Baptist?

    ?

14. Where did Jesus live until he started his lakeside ministry?

    ?

15. What religious leader was sought out by the Beatles?

    ?

Set II:

16. Felix was the governor of what ancient city?

    ?

17. What kind of wood was Noah's ark made from?

    ?

18. In the film, *The Robe,* which actor's voice was used for Christ's?

    ?

19. To what city did Jonah go to preach?

    ?

20. What is tantra?

    ?

21. Who was Abraham's nephew?

    ?

22. What religion reveres the concept of the middle path?

    ?

23. Who played a prostitute disguised as a nun in the film, *Two Mules for Sister Sara*?

    ?

24. In the Old Testament, who was the father of Ham?

    ?

25. Name the patron saint of music.

    ?

26. The *Bhagavad Gita* is the Gospel of which religion?

    ?

27. In which book of the Old Testament is there a record of Moses' farewell to Israel?

    ?

28. Although Zeus was not exactly monogamous, what was the name of his actual wife?

    ?

29. What is chanted in meditation?
?
30. Who was Benjamin's mother?
?

Set III:

31. According to the New Testament, where did Lazarus live?
?
32. In what film did Frank Sinatra play a priest?
?
33. What is the Hindu word for illusion?
?
34. Name the casket which contains the Host.
?
35. What Greek god was once a shepherd, a wolf-god, a sponsor of athletic contests, and a god of healing?
?
36. Who was the first wife of the Old Testament's King Ahasuerus?
?
37. In the Apocrypha, who was falsely accused of adultery?
?
38. Who did the Hawaiian natives worship as their volcano goddess?
?
39. Who was the mother of James and Joseph?
?
40. Who founded the "Society of Jesus"?
?
41. What religion was founded by Mrs. Glover-Patterson?
?
42. Name the attractive woman who was married to Ahab.
?
43. In what ancient city did Paul meet Lydia?
?
44. What is the Hindu word for renunciate?
?
45. Who was the mother of Timothy in the New Testament?
?

Mindbenders:

46. What Roman god was originally a protector of the fields?

?

47. "Sōtō" is a sect of which religion?

?

48. What religious group was called "The Russellites," "The Millenial Dawnists" and "The International Bible Students"?

?

49. What is the symbol of the knights who were called "Hospitalers of St. John"?

?

50. A spiritual experience called the "latian" is part of which religion?

?

Answers

Set I:

1. Dominic. He had the idea of sending his friars all over Europe to preach and teach.

2. Aristotle. St. Thomas Aquinas combined the teachings of the Greek philospher with Christian revelation.

3. Turkey. Located a short distance from Izmir, it was here that Paul told the town of Diana-worshippers that there are no gods made by hand and thereby started a riot.

4. John Huston. Huston also played the role of "Noah" in this film about the Book of Genesis.

5. A fish. It symbolizes Christianity.

6. Manna. "When the dew settled, the manna covered the

ground . . . the taste of it was like wafers made with honey" (Exodus 16:31).

7. Abraham. Revered by Moslems more than anyone else in the Bible, they consider Hebron, where Abraham is buried, to be a holy place.

8. St. Peter. Jesus told him, "Feed my lambs, feed my sheep."

9. Dionysus. During the Dionysian Festivals, the works of Aeschylus, Sophocles and Euripides were performed.

10. Buddhism. He was born in northern India around 563 B.C.

11. Germany. Born in Saxony of peasant heritage, he gave up the study of law to enter a monastery. His translations of the New Testament into German gave the Germans a uniform language for the first time.

12. Gospel of Mark. Probably written during the years 65–70 A.D., it was based on the recollections of St. Peter as set down by John Mark.

13. Elizabeth. She was Mary's cousin, and they were both expecting their first babies at the same time.

14. Nazareth. It's considered one of the three Christian cities in Palestine.

15. The Maharishi Mahesh Yogi. He became a cult hero during the sixties and was responsible for introducing transcendental meditation to the masses.

Set II:

16. Caesarea. He was soon succeeded by Porcius Festus in this important Roman city in Palestine.

17. Cypress. God told Noah to cover the cypress wood with pitch to keep out the water.

18. Cameron Mitchell. Starring Richard Burton, the film was the story of Gallio, the man responsible for carrying out Christ's execution.

19. Nineveh. It was considered a great city full of wicked people.

20. Writings. In both the Hindu and Buddhist religions, tantra are religious writings concerned with mysticism and magic.

21. Lot. Abraham traveled with him to Canaan.

22. Buddhism. The middle path is considered the path of moderation.

23. Shirley Maclaine. She co-stars with Clint Eastwood, who helps her across the Mexican desert.

24. Noah. While the Jewish faith believes that the races of the Middle East are all descended from Noah's sons, it's believed that the Hamites lived mainly in Africa.

25. Cecilia. An organ is often shown as her emblem.

26. Hinduism. This group of 100,000 couplets is also called the "Song of the Blessed Lord" and has influenced the lives of Hindu holy men, as well as Gandhi.

27. Deuteronomy. This is the fifth and final Book of Moses in the bible.

28. Hera. Their marital problems may have also been due to the fact that she was Zeus' sister.

29. Mantra. It is a word or phrase repeated internally or aloud to bring a person to Nirvana.

30. Rachel. When the youngest son of Jacob was born, as the family was traveling to Hebron, the dying Rachel named him "Ben Oni" meaning son of my sorrow. Jacob later renamed him Benjamin.

Set III:

31. Bethany. He lived with his sisters Martha and Mary.

32. *The Miracle of the Bells.* It's the story of a miracle occurring in a small coal-mining town.

33. Maya. It also means the "web of unreality."

34. Pyx. Used for blessing worshippers at certain services, it holds the wafer and is sometimes carried to the sick.

35. Apollo. Those were the god's many incarnations before he became god of the sun.

36. Vashti. He later banished her and took Esther as his second wife.

37. Susanna. When she refused the advances of two elders, she was accused of adultery and condemned to death. Young Daniel intervened and saved her.

38. Pele. It was she who made Mauna Loa erupt with fury.

39. Mary. This particular Mary was the constant companion of Mary Magdalene. She was also one of the women who gave Jesus and his disciples financial assistance and domestic help during their ministry.

40. Loyola. He was a Spanish nobleman who helped form the group of missionaries who were also called "Jesuits."

41. Christian Science. Mrs. Glover-Patterson was inspired by Dr. Quimby, a mesmerist, to become a faith-healer. Following his principles, she believed diseases and cures were a matter of faith.

42. Jezebel. A fanatical Baal worshipper, her evil deeds caught up with her and, as fate would have it, she was eaten by dogs.

43. Philippi. Lydia, who worshipped only one God, was converted and baptized by Paul.

44. *Sannyāsin*. It describes someone who renounces the world.

45. Eunice. She was a Christian Jewess married to a Greek who may have been persuaded by Paul to convert to Christianity along with Timothy.

Mindbenders:

46. Mars. He had an extremely pacifistic incarnation before he became god of war.

47. Zen Buddhism. Instead of emphasizing "what is the sound of one hand clapping," this sect's *kōan* is "just sit."

48. Jehovah's Witnesses. They were founded in 1872 by Charles Russell.

49. The Maltese Cross. Their work was to tend the sick pilgrims in Jerusalem during the Crusades.

50. Subud. Founded by Muhammed Subuh. There are over 70 Subud centers in the U.S., and groups are found in 60 countries.

MOVIES

Set I:

1. James Dean's films numbered only three: *Rebel Without a Cause, Giant* and what film based on a John Steinbeck novel?

2. In what silent classic did Charlie Chaplin eat his shoe?

3. Network was scripted by what respected writer of TV's Golden Age?

4. What nineteen-year-old ballerina became an overnight star in a Gene Kelly-Vincente Minnelli musical?

5. What was George Cukor's last film as a director?

6. What is Audrey Hepburn's physical affliction in *Wait Until Dark*?

7. What is the name of the demonic computer in the Stanley Kubrick film, *2001: A Space Odyssey*?

8. What Ingmar Bergman film later became the basis for a popular Stephen Sondheim musical?

9. Who plays the psychotic child killer in the original German version of *M*, directed by Fritz Lang?

10. What Michelangelo Antonioni film caused a scandal in the 1960s by showing Vanessa Redgrave and Sarah Miles frolicking seminude with David Hemmings?

?

11. What film provided Frank Sinatra's comeback and an Academy Award for Best Supporting Actor?

?

12. Olivia de Havilland has for many years had a famous feud with her acting sister; name this actress.

?

13. Who was MGM's first choice to play Dorothy in *The Wizard of Oz*?

?

14. In which Jeanette MacDonald/Nelson Eddy musical does Eddy play an officer of the Royal Canadian Mounted Police?

?

15. What was the name of the dog that Nick and Nora Charles owned in the "Thin Man" series of films?

?

Set II:

16. What movie was Jean Harlow making when she died of cerebral edema?

?

17. What was Judy Garland's last film for MGM?

?

18. Name the Montgomery Clift-John Wayne western made in 1948 and their only film together.

?

19. In what film does Audrey Hepburn portray an American Indian?

?

20. Who is Jean-Paul Belmondo's hero in Godard's *Breathless*?

?

21. What was the first musical made in 3-D?

?

22. Which of Fellini's films is a direct autobiographical examination of his own crisis as a creator and film director?

?

23. What's the name of the Madeline Kahn character in *Paper Moon*?

?

24. What film provided Marlon Brando with his first directing job?

?

25. In *The Bad and the Beautiful*, Gloria Grahame leaves husband Dick Powell for what Latin actor?

?

26. The Otto Preminger film, *The Moon Is Blue*, caused a scandal in 1954 by using what then-forbidden word?

?

27. What was the distinction of Disney's cartoon "Steamboat Willie"?

?

28. What film was (inaccurately) publicized by MGM as the first film in which Garbo *laughed*?

?

29. In the 1957 film musical, *The Pajama Game*, how much of a raise are the workers led by Doris Day and John Raitt striking for?

?

30. Gary Cooper won an Oscar portraying what World War I hero?

?

Set III:

31. What studio executive supervised the editing of Erich von Stroheim's *Greed* from eight hours to two hours?

?

32. What screen actress did a test for the role of Elizabeth I—to play opposite Katharine Hepburn in *Mary of Scotland*—only to be turned down because she was already known as a famous musical star?

?

33. What actor, commonly associated with Jean Cocteau, plays the Beast in Cocteau's film of *Beauty and the Beast*?

?

34. Whom did Grace Kelly replace in the title role of *The Country Girl,* which ultimately brought her an Oscar?

?

35. Who plays Spencer Tracy's sympathetic girlfriend in Fritz Lang's *Fury*?

?

36. What was Doris Day's first film?

?

37. Lee Remick took the female lead in *Anatomy of a Murder* after what prominent actress argued with director Otto Preminger and dropped out?

?

38. In what Marx Brothers movie did an unknown Marilyn Monroe make a brief appearance?

?

39. Name the important guests of honor who don't show in the comedy, *Dinner at Eight.*

?

40. What legendary star made a cameo appearance in Orson Welles's 1958 thriller, *Touch of Evil,* playing a gypsy fortune teller?

?

41. In her film debut, Ann-Margret played the daughter of what famous screen personality?

?

42. What was Clint Eastwood's first film as a director?

?

43. What song does pathetic floozy Claire Trevor sing for the amusement of her sadistic boyfriend, Edward G. Robinson, in *Key Largo*?

?

44. What does Captain Renault (Claude Rains) throw into a wastebasket in the last scene of 1943's classic, *Casablanca*?

?

45. *Mogambo,* which starred Clark Gable and Ava Gardner, was a remake of what other Clark Gable film?

?

Mindbenders:

46. *Every Sunday* was a musical short featuring Judy Garland and what other unknown child performer?

    ?

47. Luis Buñuel's *Abismos de Pasion,* made in 1953, was a modern version of what classic English novel?

    ?

48. In *Easy Living,* what falls out of a window and lands on Jean Arthur?

    ?

49. What is the profession of Lillian Gish's father—played by Donald Crisp—in the 1919 classic, *Broken Blossoms*?

    ?

50. In the William Wyler film, *Friendly Persuasion,* what does Dorothy McGuire insist husband Gary Cooper must keep in the attic?

    ?

Answers

Set I:

1. *East of Eden.* Dean received an Oscar nomination for his performance in this film.

2. *The Gold Rush.* In this 1925 comedy, Chaplin's Tramp became a prospector.

3. Paddy Chayefsky. He also wrote the Oscar-winning *Marty.*

4. Leslie Caron. She was handpicked for her role in *An American in Paris* by Kelly.

5. *Rich and Famous.* This 1982 film starred Jacqueline Bisset and Candice Bergen.

6. Blindness. This handicap heightened the tension as she was pursued in her own home by killers.

7. "Hal." This machine plots with varying degrees of success against astronauts Keir Dullea and Gary Lockwood.

8. *Smiles of a Summer Night.* It inspired the Broadway musical *A Little Night Music.*

9. Peter Lorre. He established his international reputation by this role.

10. *Blow-Up.* The film was condemned by the Catholic Church in 1967.

11. *From Here to Eternity.* The 1953 hit film based on the best-selling novel by James Jones also brought an Oscar to Donna Reed.

12. Joan Fontaine. She reportedly aroused de Havilland's wrath by beating her out for the Oscar in 1941 when she won for *Suspicion.*

13. Shirley Temple. She overshadowed Judy Garland then as the most popular child star in films, but her studio, 20th Century-Fox, wanted too much money for her.

14. *Rose Marie.* In this 1938 film, they sing the then-very-popular "Indian Love Call."

15. Asta. He was a handsome wire-haired terrier.

Set II:

16. *Saratoga.* She was starring with Clark Gable in this 1937 film.

17. *Summer Stock.* She appeared for the last time with Gene Kelly.

18. *Red River.* This was also Clift's first film.

19. *The Unforgiven.* She is adopted by Burt Lancaster and family in this 1960 John Huston western.

20. Humprey Bogart. Bogart's style and films are satirized in this example of the French New Wave.

21. *Kiss Me Kate*. Released in 1953 by MGM, it starred Kathryn Grayson and Howard Keel.

22. *8½*. It was voted Best Foreign Film of 1963 by the Academy of Motion Picture Arts and Sciences.

23. Trixie Delight. She plays Ryan O'Neil's bubble-headed girl friend in the 1972 film.

24. *One-Eyed Jacks*. This controversial 1960 western was originally to have been directed by Stanley Kubrick.

25. Gilbert Roland. He played the part of "Gaucho," and they both pay for their infidelity, incidentally, by dying in a plane crash.

26. "Virgin." This one word prevented the film from getting a Production Code seal—but not an audience.

27. Sound. Made in 1928, the cartoon also presented Mickey Mouse in his third appearance.

28. *Ninotchka*. In this 1939 comedy, Melvyn Douglas melts the cold exterior of the Soviet comrade played by Garbo.

29. Seven and one-half cents. This was the title of the big production number, and the original title of the book that the play was based on.

30. *Sergeant York*. This 1941 film brought Cooper the first of his two Best Actor Oscars.

Set III:

31. Irving Thalberg. He has long been accused of damaging one of the masterpieces of the American cinema.

32. Ginger Rogers. She finally made the transition to serious acting in the 1940 film, *Kitty Foyle*.

33. Jean Marais. He also appeared in Cocteau's *Two-Headed Eagle* and *Les Parents Terribles*.

34. Jennifer Jones. She had become pregnant before production started.

35. Sylvia Sidney. It was Lang's first film made in America.

36. *Romance on the High Seas*. This 1949 frothy musical had been originally intended for Judy Garland.

37. Lana Turner. Her career in 1959 was in an upswing after her great success in *Peyton Place*.

38. *Love Happy*. Produced in 1949, it was the final film collaboration of the Marx Brothers.

39. Lord and Lady Ferncliff. These were the people that the Jean Harlow character, Kitty Packard, was dying to impress.

40. Marlene Dietrich. She made this fresh from her great success in *Witness for the Prosecution*.

41. Bette Davis. She played "Apple Annie" in 1961's *A Pocketful of Miracles* and posed as a society matron for her visiting daughter.

42. *Play Misty for Me*. The 1971 film popularized the song, "The First Time Ever I Saw Your Face."

43. "Moanin' Low." Trevor won a Best Supporting Actress Oscar for this 1948 film role.

44. A bottle of Vichy water. This gesture indicated Renault's rupture with the Nazi-allied Vichy government.

45. *Red Dust*. This 1932 film teamed Gable with Jean Harlow in the Gardner role.

Mindbenders:

46. Deanna Durbin. She was to become a huge musical star for Universal in the thirties and forties.

47. *Wuthering Heights*. The novel was also filmed in 1920, 1939, and 1970.

48. Mink coat. This device sets the action in motion of this Depression-era comedy.

49. Boxer. His outbursts of physical violence end up costing Miss Gish her life.

50. Organ. He bought the instrument at the state fair, but it was forbidden by their strict Quaker religion.

BUSINESS, PRODUCTS AND MONEY

Set I:

1. Who is the first female to appear on a U.S. coin?
   ?
2. What millionaire was killed when the Titanic hit the iceberg?
   ?
3. How many herbs and spices are used in Kentucky Fried Chicken?
   ?
4. What coin features the likeness of Monticello?
   ?
5. What's the name of the awards given by Senator William Proxmire for wasteful government spending?
   ?
6. According to their advertising slogan, what products are "indescribably delicious"?
   ?
7. Who financed Columbus's voyages to America?
   ?
8. How much did Michelle Triola Marvin win in her very first lawsuit against her longtime live-in lover, Lee Marvin?
   ?
9. In the "Does she or doesn't she" ads, what is it that "only her hairdresser knows for sure"?
   ?
10. What prescription drug is prescribed more than any others?
    ?
11. What did Richard Nixon do to the dollar in 1973?
    ?

12. Which state has the most millionaires?

?

13. Considering the fact that the Teddy bear is one of the world's biggest-selling dolls, for whom was the doll originally named?

?

14. What one appliance is found in nearly every American home?

?

15. Name the nationally known accounting firm that's responsible for tallying the votes at the Academy Awards.

?

Set II:

16. What popular toy did Barbara Handler inspire?

?

17. Who invented Tupperware?

?

18. What's the biggest-selling candy bar in the U.S.?

?

19. What does "A & P" stand for?

?

20. If the nation's gold is at Fort Knox, where's the country's silver?

?

21. What newspaper has "all the news that's fit to print"?

?

22. What country has the world's fastest train?

?

23. What's the largest industry in the United States?

?

24. If you're hungry and travelling across the country, which fast food chain would you encounter the most?

?

25. What industry employs the most people in the U.S.?

?

26. What was the very first product to incorporate a jingle in its advertising?

?

27. Although famous for establishing the Nobel Peace Prize,

Alfred Nobel amassed his fortune after inventing what commodity?

?

28. What were the first words ever telegraphed?

?

29. What's the world's largest department store under one roof?

?

30. Which hotel chain is the most successful?

?

Set III:

31. Who started the first mail-order house?

?

32. Why did Rene Lacoste put a crocodile on his famous sports shirts?

?

33. What U.S. port handles the most tonnage of shipping per year?

?

34. What was the nation's first mass produced automobile?

?

35. At what company was the first black sit-in held to protest segregation?

?

36. Who invented the potato chip?

?

37. How long is the average U.S. grocery shopping trip?

?

38. What's the largest single food item imported into the United States?

?

39. Name the French fashion designer who was once a disciple of Balenciaga and a former assistant to Schiaparelli.

?

40. Which city has the highest per capita auto theft rate?

?

41. Which U.S. company is the most philanthropic?

?

42. What airline has the most passengers?

?

43. Which state has the most millionaires per 1,000 population?

?

44. How much was the first minimum wage in America?

?

45. Which company spends the most on research per year?

?

Mindbenders:

46. What's the first product ever advertised in the United States?

?

47. What is the most valuable comic book in the U.S. today?

?

48. What American financier had the middle name of "Fortune"?

?

49. Whose likeness was on the first postage stamp in the U.S.?

?

50. What is the largest number in the world?

?

Answers

Set I:

1. Susan B. Anthony. The dollar coin with her likeness is often confused with the half-dollar and never became popular.

2. John Jacob Astor. His great-grandfather amassed the family fortune in the fur trade, and the Oregon city of Astoria was named after him.

3. Eleven. That number is according to the company's television commercial.

4. Nickel. Besides designing Monticello, Jefferson was also responsible for the design of Washington, D.C. along with Pierre L'Enfant.

5. Golden Fleece Awards. Announcing these awards periodically, the senator is trying to minimize governmental grants for dubious studies.

6. Peter Paul candy bars. Despite the slogan, Peter Paul's Almond Joy is thirteenth in candy bar sales and the company's Mounds is fifteenth.

7. King Ferdinand V and Queen Isabella I. They also expelled the Jews from Spain and put the Inquisition under royal control.

8. $104,000. This famous lawsuit brought the word "palimony" into our vocabulary.

9. Dye her hair. During the run of this famous campaign, the commercials had a child in every one in order to add respectability to them.

10. Valium. The drug is one of Roche Laboratories' most profitable products.

11. Devalued the dollar. Besides devaluating the currency by 10 percent, he also imposed wage-and-price controls.

12. New York. At last count, New York has 51,031 millionaires while runner-up California has only 33,509.

13. Theodore Roosevelt. Often identified with the great outdoors, Roosevelt fathered important conservation legislation.

14. Toaster. This appliance is found in 99.9 percent of all American homes.

15. Price-Waterhouse. The firm has been counting the Academy's votes since 1935.

Set II:

16. Barbie doll. It was designed by her mother and manufactured by Mattel. The Barbie doll celebrated her twenty-fifth birthday on May 17, 1983.

17. Earl Tupper. A chemist at DuPont, he used plastics and an inverted paint can lid to develop an airtight container during the late 1940s.

18. Snickers Bar. It's made by the Mars Candy Company which, along with Hershey Company, are responsible for nine of the ten top-selling candy bars in the country.

19. Atlantic and Pacific Tea Company. When the company began in 1835, it sold only coffee and tea.

20. West Point. Besides being the site of the United States Military Academy since 1802, this city on the Hudson River was an important fort during the Revolutionary War.

21. *New York Times*. Although probably the most prominent newspaper in our country, it's still outsold in New York City by the *Daily News*.

22. France. The TGV trains between Paris and the south cover a distance of 225½ miles and attain an average speed of 112 miles per hour.

23. Food industry. Americans spend $250 billion each year on food—or $1,000 for every man, woman and child.

24. Kentucky Fried Chicken. At last count, there are 5,355 Kentucky Fried Chicken stores versus 5,185 McDonald's Hamburger units.

25. Restaurant industry. Four million people nationwide are employed in restaurants.

26. Wrigley's gum. Written in 1926 by Billy Rose, it was entitled, "Does Your Spearmint Lose Its Flavor on the Bedpost Overnight?" and later became a hit novelty record in 1961.

27. Dynamite. So concerned about the potential abuses of the explosives he invented, the Swedish chemist set up his annual awards to promote peace and a greater civilization.

28. "What hath God wrought." These words were telegraphed by Samuel F.B. Morse in May, 1844.

29. Marshall Field's in Chicago. Amassing one of the largest private fortunes in America, the store's founder, Marshall Field, also was one of the founders of Chicago's Art Institute and Museum of Natural History.

30. Holiday Inn. This chain's sales are twice the number of its nearest competitor, Sheraton Hotels.

Set III:

31. Montgomery Ward. He turned his profitable business into a series of stores.

32. His nickname was "crocodile." The famous French tennis player was dubbed "the crocodile" because of his large nose. He broke tradition by wearing colored shirts on the courts.

33. New Orleans. It handled over 188 million tons at last count. Next is New York with 156 million, and third is Houston at almost 101 million tons of shipping.

34. Ford Model N. Depressed by the poor sales of his Model K, which was a limousine selling for $2,500, Henry Ford brought out the Model N to sell for $500. Ford utilized all of these hard-learned lessons when he manufactured his classic Model T.

35. Woolworth's. It occurred at the lunch counter on February 1, 1960 in Greensboro, North Carolina.

36. George Crum. Serving as chef of a Sarasota resort in 1853, he answered a customer's complaint about the thickness of his french fries with potatoes cut as thin as possible.

37. Thirty-one minutes. The average female shopper spends approximately $1.07 per minute.

38. Coffee. Four billion dollars' worth a year is imported.

39. Hubert de Givenchy. Opening his own fashion house in 1952, he set standards of elegance with his print fabrics, evening clothes, and sleeveless coats.

40. Boston. With 16.48 cars stolen out of every 1,000, the city has the highest auto theft insurance rates.

41. Exxon. In one year, the corporation contributed $27.6 million to various causes. The company is also ranked number one on the Fortune Five Hundred list with sales of $88.6 billion.

42. Eastern Airlines. Even though Eastern flew the most passengers last year, the airline wasn't as profitable as third-ranked United Airlines.

43. Idaho. There are 26.65 millionaires per 1,000 people.

44. Twenty-five cents an hour. This was established by Congress in 1938.

45. General Motors. The company spent $1.9 billion in one year. The next highest spenders on research are Ford and IBM.

Mindbenders:

46. Advertising. On April 17, 1704, the *Boston Newsletter* advertised for advertising. By May 1, it was printing its first ad for real estate.

47. Marvel Comic #1. Introduced in October, 1939, this premiere issue featured the Human Torch and was selling recently for $13,500.

48. Thomas Fortune Ryan. Besides acquiring millions, he also dominated the New York City public transportation industry and co-founded the American Tobacco Company.

49. Benjamin Franklin. The stamp cost a nickel and was issued on July 1, 1847.

50. Centillion. There are three hundred and three zeroes following the first digit.

ART AND ARCHITECTURE

Set I:

1. Name the artist who made "drip paintings" famous.

    ?

2. Besides Doric and Corinthian, what is the third style of Greek column?

    ?

3. Who is the world's best-known Surrealist painter?

    ?

4. What are the catacombs?

    ?

5. What is an amphora?

    ?

6. What's the name of the former warehouse area in New York City that now contains artists' lofts and galleries?

    ?

7. Name the Norwegian artist who painted *The Scream*.

    ?

8. For what reason was the Temple of Delphi in Greece best known?

    ?

9. What is a serigraph?

    ?

10. Who is the most famous nature photographer of our time?

    ?

11. Why is it that many fifteen-story buildings don't contain fifteen stories?

    ?

12. What modern designer became famous by reproducing the opalescent sheen seen on ancient Egyptian glass?

?

13. What ex-patriate American writer and art collector was a close personal friend of both Picasso and Matisse?

?

14. In front of what Roman monument do tourists perform a custom that's said to insure their return?

?

15. In what museum will you find the Mona Lisa?

?

Set II:

16. Although originally entitled *The Company of Captain Frans Banning Cocq*, this famous Rembrandt painting is better known by what name?

?

17. What twentieth century head of state was also a prolific and accomplished painter?

?

18. Name the early Renaissance artist who was also a monk.

?

19. What's the term that encompasses Aztec, Mayan, Incan and early North American Indian art?

?

20. What was Whistler's nationality?

?

21. Name the powerful and wealthy Italian Renaissance family who were the greatest art patrons of their era.

?

22. Who designed the Brooklyn Bridge?

?

23. Pointillism is most often associated with what artist?

?

24. In the mid-nineteenth century, what artist began the trend of Pre-Raphaelite art in England?

?

25. Who designed *The Gateway Arch* in St. Louis?

?

26. Name the Northern Renaissance artist who glorified the art of engraving and woodcuts.

?

27. Which Greek island is well known as an artists' colony?

?

28. Who coined the term "shocking pink"?

?

29. What part of a cathedral is the nave?

?

30. With what ancient civilization is the minotaur artistically associated?

?

Set III:

31. What U.S. museum is a replica of an ancient Roman villa?

?

32. What small city in France is world famous for its artists' tapestries?

?

33. Name the artist who painted the fantasy triptych, *The Garden of Delights*.

?

34. What are the Elgin Marbles?

?

35. What twentieth-century painter was made Commissar of Fine Arts in Russia?

?

36. The original murals in New York's Rockefeller Center were executed by what artist?

?

37. Who invented the stabile?

?

38. What Spanish painter was deaf?

?

39. Name the futuristic city being built by the architect, Paolo Soleri.

?

40. To what substance was Toulouse-Lautrec addicted?

?

41. Although well-known for his nude studies, what photographer is most famous for his shots of a nautilus shell?

?

42. Name the landscape architect who designed Central Park in New York City.

?

43. Small display boxes containing three-dimensional collages made with everyday objects are known by what name?

?

44. Besides painting, Matisse is best remembered for what other art form?

?

45. What European architect is best known for his intricate, ornate buildings that sometimes resemble wedding cakes?

?

Mindbenders:

46. What large church was originally constructed without any nails?

?

47. Name the contemporary artist who wrapped the coast of Australia in parachute fabric.

?

48. John Sloan and Robert Henri were part of what American artistic movement?

?

49. Which art scholar wrote the first definitive history of art?

?

50. What is a maquette?

?

Answers

Set I:

1. Jackson Pollock. He dripped paint on continuous lengths of canvas and cut them into paintings after they dried.

2. Ionic. Named for the Greek architectural order of which it was a part, this column is topped with a scroll design.

3. Salvador Dali. Named by Appollinaire, the Surrealist movement became famous largely because of Dali's theatricality.

4. Subterranean Roman tombs. Decorated with paintings, these vaults were used by early Christians to bury their dead.

5. Greek jar. This storage jar with two handles was used for wine or oil.

6. Soho. The art revival began there in the sixties and became semi-official with the opening of the Paula Cooper Gallery in 1968.

7. Edvard Munch. An expressionist painter, much of Munch's work was frenzied and hysterical.

8. Oracle. The Delphic oracle was alleged to have given ambiguous advice in ancient Greece.

9. Silkscreen. Begun in the 1930s, the technique utilizes a squeegee to push paint through a screen, with a separate screen for each color.

10. Ansel Adams. He perfected a precision of light and dark in his breathtaking black and white photographs of U.S. national parks.

11. No thirteenth floor. Many architechts and tenants are super-stitious.

12. Louis Tiffany. His Favrile glass was designed to look like the glass that had been buried in tombs and with which natural minerals had interacted.

13. Gertrude Stein. She and her brother, Leo, nurtured and collected many of the greatest modern artists in their Paris home.

14. Trevi Fountain. Coins that are tossed over one's shoulder into the fountain are said to guarantee that person's return visit.

15. The Louvre. It is guarded at all times in the Paris museum and protected by a special temperature-control gauge.

Set II:

16. *The Night Watch*. Within this group portrait of local defense volunteers in Amsterdam, each model was paid by his position in the painting.

17. Winston Churchill. Not only was he a great leader and artist, but his writing won him a Nobel Prize in 1953.

18. Fra Filippo Lippi. He eventually left the monastery and abducted a nun whom he later married.

19. Pre-Columbian. It literally refers to all the art in the Americas created before Columbus's voyage.

20. American. James Abbott McNeill Whistler was born in Massachusetts in 1834, studied art in Paris and once sued an art critic for saying that he had "flung a pot of paint in the public's face."

21. Medici. They commissioned much of Michelangelo's work.

22. John Roebling. He died during its construction, but his son supervised the bridge's completion in 1883.

23. Georges Seurat. Having a scientific interest in light and vision, he wanted to recreate how our eyes break light into colors.

24. Dante Gabriel Rossetti. He and his group reacted to what they called the "overpraised and insincere" work of Raphael.

25. Eero Saarinen. The Finnish-born architect designed the arch for a competition in 1948 and completed it in 1964.

26. Albrecht Durer. Among his best-known works were *Adam and Eve* and *Knight, Death and the Devil.*

27. Mykonos. Artists come from all over the world to take advantage of the special quality of the light found on the island.

28. Schiaparelli. She invented the color for her designs.

29. Central aisle. In this cruciform style of building, it's the main aisle leading to the altar.

30. Crete. The ruins of the Palace of Knossos contain a maze of corridors associated with the famous legend.

Set III:

31. Getty Museum. Situated on a Los Angeles hillside overlooking the Pacific, the building was modeled after the ancient Villa of Papyri which was destroyed by the eruption of Vesuvius in 79 A.D.

32. Aubusson. Picasso, Miro and Chagall have taken their paintings there to be made into tapestries by the master weavers.

33. Hieronymous Bosch. The fifteenth-century Dutch painter depicted an obsessive Gothic fantasy of heaven, earth and hell in minute detail.

34. Greek sculpture. Removed from the Parthenon by Lord Elgin in 1801 and presently displayed at London's British Museum, the sculpture is now being sought by the Greek government for return to Athens.

35. Marc Chagall. Although his colorful, fantasy style was formed in his Russian village home, he's spent most of his life in Paris.

36. Diego Rivera. The Mexican painter used as his subject the class struggles of his people.

37. Alexander Calder. Originally an engineer, Calder married sculpture and engineering by creating this form.

38. Goya. Coming in his middle age, Goya's deafness motivated him to expand from portrait painting to more socially relevant themes.

39. Arcosanti. Being built by volunteers in the Arizona desert, this city of tomorrow is far from completion and usually in need of funding.

40. Absinthe. After having developed an addiction to this liqueur derived from wormwood and anise, the artist suffered from the DT's and died at the age of thirty-seven.

41. Edward Weston. He particularly enjoyed shooting nature.

42. Frederick Olmsted. Considered America's greatest landscape architect, he completed the park in 1858, basing much of it on his Audubon Park in New Orleans.

43. Cornell box. This art form was invented by Joseph Cornell.

44. Paper cutouts. Compensating for the handicaps of age and illness, he did the cutouts in the last stages of his career.

45. Antonio Gaudi. Some of his works have been described as whimsical sand castles.

Mindbenders:

46. Mormon Tabernacle. Constructed in Salt Lake City, some of the building's newer wings are now built with nails.

47. Christo. A conceptual artist, this artist believes in bringing art, people and their landscape together in an effort to keep art alive.

48. Ashcan School. Started by newspaper illustrators using journalistic subjects, this group of nineteenth- and twentieth-century realist painters was also known as "The Eight."

49. Giorgio Vasari. Written in 1560, Vasari's *Lives* showed the rise, fall and rebirth of art from ancient Rome through the dark ages and up to Michelangelo.

50. Sculptor's miniature. Essentially, it's a very rough, miniature version that the sculptor makes of a larger work in progress.

MEDICINE AND HEALTH

Set I:

1. What food group supplies most of the body's energy?
   ?

2. What are hemorrhoids?
   ?

3. A high cholesterol level in the blood allegedly causes what serious disease?
   ?

4. What causes warts?
   ?

5. A stroke is caused when the blood supply is cut off to what part of the body?
   ?

6. What is agoraphobia?
   ?

7. In the Middle Ages, to whom did the common people go for medical care?
   ?

8. Besides the lymph glands, what other organ produces lymphocytes?
   ?

9. The lower number in a blood pressure reading is known by what name?
   ?

10. What crippling, thousand-year-old practice was forbidden by the Manchu conquerors of China in the nineteenth century?
    ?

11. Who is considered to be the greatest physician of all time?

?

12. Who tended to the health of primitive peoples in northern Europe and Asia?

?

13. Considered to be the most common form of color blindness is the inability to distinguish between what two colors?

?

14. Who designed the artificial heart that was implanted in Dr. Barney Clark?

?

15. From what other blood vessel is a coronary artery bypass made?

?

Set II:

16. When a part of the stomach strikes up through the abdomen and into the chest, this condition is called by what name?

?

17. Approximately how long is the small intestine?

?

18. What is the cause of most kidney stones?

?

19. What causes a bruise to fade away?

?

20. What is Type II diabetes?

?

21. Approximately what percent of the human body is water?

?

22. For a regular smoker, how much life expectancy is lost with each cigarette?

?

23. Name the cancer that occurs in bone or muscle tissue.

?

24. Where is the parietal bone located?

?

25. How long does it take new skin cells to reach the surface of the skin?

?

26. Of the people who try to commit suicide, what percentage of them actually succeed?

?

27. What human body part did some American Indian medicine men use for a medicine bag?

?

28. What causes the body to go into shock?

?

29. How did the Black Death spread to Western Europe?

?

30. Name the condition that makes "little old ladies (and men)" little.

?

Set III:

31. What is cystitis?

?

32. What do the letters C.A.T. stand for in "CAT scan"?

?

33. What was believed to be the cause of dental disease in ancient Egypt?

?

34. What is the Ospedale degli Innocenti?

?

35. Who was the father of comparative anatomy?

?

36. What does the mitral valve control?

?

37. What healing theory used today was developed by Daniel D. Palmer?

?

38. Where does the symbol of the Red Cross come from?

?

39. Who was the first woman to graduate from an American medical school?

?

40. Why should children with viral illnesses *not* be given aspirin?

?

41. What is a CVA?

?

42. Name the disease that afflicted the Elephant Man.

    ?

43. How big is a nine-week-old fetus?

    ?

44. What is septicimia?

    ?

45. Considered to be the basis of Greek and medieval medicine, the "four humors" consisted of blood, yellow bile, black bile and what other bodily substance?

    ?

Mindbenders:

46. Who invented the ambulance?

    ?

47. What was Dr. William Harvey's immortal contribution to medicine?

    ?

48. Who was considered to be the greatest surgeon of the Renaissance period?

    ?

49. Who is considered to be the father of American psychiatry?

    ?

50. What was Dr. Sigmund Freud's medical specialty?

    ?

Answers

Set I:

1. Carbohydrates. They are the source of 50 percent of the body's energy.

2. Varicose veins in the anus. People in sedentary jobs are more prone to this condition.

3. Arteriosclerosis. This condition leads to heart attacks and strokes.

4. Virus. It causes skin cells to multiply rapidly, causing the growth.

5. Brain. It may be caused by a cerebral thrombosis (arterial clot), cerebral embolism (foreign object stuck in the artery) or cerebral hemorrhage (burst artery).

6. Fear of open spaces. Some agoraphobics cannot leave their homes without suffering acute anxiety attacks.

7. Barber. While trained physicians cared for the upper classes, the barber performed blood-letting, tooth-pulling, surgery, bone-setting, and occasionally, hair-cutting.

8. Spleen. Lymphocytes are white blood cells that aid the body's immune system.

9. Diastolic. The upper number, systolic pressure, is when the heart contracts to pump out blood, while diastolic pressure is when the heart relaxes to let in blood.

10. Foot binding. Originally a method to keep wives close to home, it was performed by compressing the toe and heel and bandaging them tightly.

11. Hippocrates. Flourishing between 460 and 370 B.C., he was renowned for his collection of treatises, *Corpus Hippocraticum,* his rational, empiric methods and the Hippocratic Oath.

12. Shaman. He was also responsible for religion, warding off catastrophes and the weather.

13. Red and green. Total color blindness is very rare.

14. Dr. Robert Jarvik. Dr. Clark lived for 112 days with the Jarvik-7 plastic heart.

15. Vein from the leg. These vessels have proved more successful in adapting to the heart's circulation.

Set II:

16. Hiatus hernia. It can be controlled by medication.

17. Sixteen to twenty-one feet. The small intestine absorbs nutrients from food.

18. Too much calcium in the urine. Passing kidney stones is said to cause the most excruciating pain known to man.

19. White blood cells. The bruise is broken down by these cells which are also called monocytes.

20. Noninsulin-dependent diabetes. This condition is eight times more common than insulin-dependent (Type I) diabetes.

21. Fifty percent. We lose four pints of water per day in sweat, urine and exhalation.

22. Five and a half minutes. The average smoker is fourteen times more likely to die of lung cancer and twice as likely to die of a heart attack than a nonsmoker.

23. Sarcoma. Unlike carcinomas, which develop in the skin, glands and organs are often curable if found in the early stages, sarcomas are rare and difficult to treat.

24. Skull. Located at the back of the head, it's one of the twenty-six bones that form the skull.

25. One month. The epidermis is completely replaced every thirty days.

26. Ten percent. In the U.S. approximately 200,000 people attempt suicide each year, and about 22,000 succeed.

27. Scrotum. It was assumed to have healing powers.

28. Drop in blood pressure. When this happens, the flow of blood and its oxygen supply to the vital organs become inadequate.

29. By the Crusaders. Returning from the Middle East, the Crusaders brought bubonic plague with them which wiped out one quarter of Europe's population between 1347 and 1348.

30. Osteoporosis. Known as brittle bone disease, this condition leads to hip and vertebral fractures, but it's easily preventable if adequate calcium is supplied in the diet.

Set III:

31. Bladder infection. It's more common in women because the female urethra is comparatively short, making it easier for bacteria from the outside to reach the bladder.

32. Computerized axial tomography. This type of X ray is used to show a cross-section of the brain and other difficult-to-photograph areas.

33. Worms. This idea persisted in many areas until the eighteenth century.

34. Oldest children's hospital. It was founded in Florence in 1419.

35. Aristotle. His work still influences today's physicians.

36. Blood flow in the left side of the heart. Blood moves from the left atrium through the mitral valve into the left ventricle.

37. Chiropractic. It treats illnesses through manipulation of the spine and other body structures.

38. Swiss flag. Swiss-born Jean Henri Dunant founded the Red Cross and chose its symbol as a reverse of the flag. He won the first Nobel Peace Prize in 1901.

39. Dr. Elizabeth Blackwell. Receiving her degree in 1849, she passed the qualifying exam with the highest grade in her class at the Geneva College of Medicine in New York.

40. Reye's Syndrome. This deadly disease seems to develop in children who have such viral diseases as chicken pox or influenza when they take aspirin.

41. Cerebrovascular accident. This is the medical term for a stroke.

42. Neurofibromatosis. An inherited condition that affects the skin, muscles, skeleton and nervous system, it's characterized by soft, multiple tumors distributed all over the body.

43. About one and one-fourth inches. At this stage, the fetus is becoming recognizably human.

44. Blood poisoning. It's caused by a bacterial infection in the bloodstream.

45. Phlegm. They believed that blood evaporated in the lungs and was exhaled, yellow bile made one irritable, black bile made one sad and phlegm was produced in the brain.

Mindbenders:

46. Dominique-Jean Larrey. This French surgeon thought of using wagons to carry the wounded off the battlefields during the Napoleonic wars.

47. Explanation of the circulatory system. He proved that the blood in our bodies was continually recirculating.

48. Ambroise Paré. He wrote the influential *A Universal Surgery* which was based on his treatment of battle wounds.

49. Benjamin Rush. He was one of the signers of the Declaration of Independence and author of the first American book on psychiatry, published in 1812.

50. Neurology. He was fascinated by all the medical specialties.

CLASSICAL MUSIC AND OPERA

Set I:

1. What classical composer wrote 104 symphonies?

    ?

2. Aram Khachaturian's music draws upon the folk songs of what former country?

    ?

3. Johann Sebastian Bach was afflicted with what physical disability?

    ?

4. The opera, *Aida,* was commissioned to honor what event?

    ?

5. In Gustav Holst's *The Planets,* which planet is "The Bringer of War?"

    ?

6. Beethoven dubbed what kind of composition his *Pathétique*?

    ?

7. Chopin was extremely loyal and nationalistic toward what country?

    ?

8. Modest Mussorgsky's work was reorchestrated and softened by what other composer?

    ?

9. Aaron Copland used cowboy songs in what orchestral/ballet work?

    ?

10. Which work by Stravinsky caused a now-legendary riot in the audience on the night it premiered?

    ?

11. "The Titan" is a nickname for the first symphony of which composer?

?

12. In an opera, what do you call the dialogue between arias?

?

13. What was the number of Schubert's "Unfinished Symphony"?

?

14. The "Liebestod" or "Love Death" is the stunning final aria of what opera by Wagner?

?

15. Bach and Handel composed at the end of what musical era?

?

Set II:

16. The Henry James novella *The Turn of the Screw* was turned into an opera by what British composer?

?

17. By what name is Mozart's Symphony Number 41 in C major known?

?

18. *Pelléas et Mélisande* is the only opera of what important European composer?

?

19. *The Thousand and One Arabian Nights* inspired what musical outing by both Ravel and Rimsky-Korsakov?

?

20. The use of recurrent signature melodies—leitmotifs—is most strongly identified with what composer of opera?

?

21. Debussy's *Suite Bergamasque* contains what famous example of his piano works?

?

22. The poem *Ode to Joy,* which is set to music in Beethoven's final symphony, the Ninth, was written by what poet?

?

23. What is the occupation of the heroine in Puccini's *Tosca*?

?

24. What Mahler work is based on a cycle of six Chinese poems?

?

25. What American composer worked in insurance, created his music in obscurity for forty years, and scorned the Pulitzer Prize that was awarded to him shortly before his death?

?

26. What is the name of the corrupt Venetian courtesan who betrays the hero in the second tale of Offenbach's *Tales of Hoffmann*?

?

27. What famous composer discovered the Symphony #9 in C major by Schubert?

?

28. Which of Bach's sons developed the sonata form?

?

29. The opera, *Cavalleria Rusticana* is most often performed in tandem with what other well-known opera?

?

30. Which symphony of Rachmaninoff's opened to such critical distaste that the composer thought his career was over?

?

Set III:

31. Romantic composer Franz Schubert died as a result of what disease?

?

32. What was Puccini's last *complete* opera?

?

33. The K numbers, developed by Austrian naturalist Ludwig von Koechel, are used to identify what composer's works?

?

34. Popular French writer Colette created a delightful libretto for an opera by what composer?

?

35. For whom are Gregorian chants named?

?

36. What opera broke the tradition of grand opera by setting the action in the present with contemporary constuming?

?

37. What French composer was also a doctor of medicine?

?

38. What is the name of Beethoven's patron—to whom he dedicated a famous sonata?

?

39. What is the name of Pinkerton's ship in *Madama Butterfly*?

?

40. Modest Mussorgsky, Nikolai Rimsky-Korsakov, Cesar Cui, Alexander Borodin and what other composer made up the group of Russian nationalists labeled "The Five"?

?

41. What composer believed the full moon was harmful and refused to see visitors when the moon was full in March and September?

?

42. What composer uttered the word *Tristan* as his last before his death?

?

43. Alban Berg was the most famous student of what Expressionist composer?

?

44. The famous and often satirized character of Brunnhilde first appeared in what Wagner opera?

?

45. What was Stravinsky's first *full-length* opera?

?

Mindbenders:

46. What contemporary composer created the twelve-tone scale?

?

47. What artist created the paintings that inspired Moussorgsky's *Pictures at an Exhibition*?

?

48. Jacopo Peri and Giulio Caccini are credited with the composition of the *very first* opera in 1594; what is its title?

?

49. What German composer was only a twelve-year-old prodigy when seventy-two-year-old Goethe was his playmate?

?

50. The earliest known instrumental music was written in what civilization?

?

Answers

Set I:

1. Josef Haydn. The next most prolific symphony composer after Haydn would be Mozart, who wrote forty-one.

2. Armenia. It was Khachaturian's homeland.

3. Blindness. Apparently, it was induced from his copying of manuscripts by moonlight as a boy.

4. Opening of the Suez Canal. Because of political reasons, the premiere was delayed by two years to 1871.

5. Mars. This is one of seven planets musically invoked in this suite.

6. Sonata. It was Tchaikovsky who wrote the *Pathétique* Symphony.

7. Poland. It was his native land and for which he composed some of his most stirring music.

8. Nikolai Rimsky-Korsakov. His orchestrations have recently been revoked in favor of Mussorgsky's originals when available.

9. *Billy the Kid.* Cowboy songs were also used in his ballet *Rodeo.*

10. *The Rite of Spring.* Although the 1913 Paris audience tore the theater apart, Stravinsky's work blazed the trail for new musical idioms.

11. Gustav Mahler. He claimed the symphony was a recreation of "the sound of nature."

12. Recitative. It is accompanied by a musical background.

13. Eighth. He wrote a ninth and a tenth—both of which were discovered posthumously.

14. *Tristan und Isolde*. The opera is based on an English legend as old as the legend of King Arthur.

15. Baroque. The music featured solo instruments and sought to express the affections of the human soul such as anger, grandeur and heroism.

Set II:

16. Benjamin Britten. His other famous opera is *Peter Grimes*.

17. *Jupiter*. Although Mozart was under financial stress, he composed this monumental work in a period of six weeks.

18. Debussy. The work had its premiere in 1902.

19. *Scheherezade*. Both composers used the story as an orchestral work.

20. Wagner. He systematized the leitmotif far beyond any of his precursors or contemporaries.

21. "Clair de Lune." It's very popular as an encore among piano soloists.

22. Schiller. He was regarded as the foremost German Romantic poet.

23. Singer. She sings at a victory dinner celebrating the defeat of Napoleon by the Italians.

24. *Das Lied von der Erde*. Musicologists consider this piece to be Mahler's true Tenth Symphony.

25. Charles Ives. His progressive music anticipated the changes of the twentieth century.

26. Giulietta. She and Olympia, Stella and Antonia—all love objects in the same opera—are usually performed by the same diva.

27. Robert Schumann. He found the symphony among some of Schubert's belongings that his brother had saved ten years after Schubert's death.

28. Carl Philip Emanuel Bach. He had a great influence on both Mozart and Haydn.

29. *I Pagliacci.* Both operas are examples of the Italian "verismo" style which focused on the lives of ordinary people.

30. First. Although his anxiety almost precluded his writing a second, Rachmaninoff's Second Symphony was indeed a success.

Set III:

31. Syphilis. Although many sources list the cause of death as typhoid fever because of a Viennese epidemic at that time, it's been recently corroborated that he died from a sexually transmitted disease.

32. *Il Trittico. Turandot,* which is usually thought to be Puccini's last opera, was completed by Franco Alfano after Puccini's death.

33. Mozart. The K numbers were mandatory since many of his works were published without opus numbers or with incorrect chronological listings.

34. Ravel. They collaborated on *L'Enfant et les Sortileges* in 1925.

35. Pope Gregory I. In the sixth century, he decreed that all hitherto vocal music collected in the Church be coded and put on paper.

36. *La Traviata.* Composed by Verdi, the opera was an adaptation of the very popular *Camille* by Alexandre Dumas fils.

37. Hector Berlioz. Forced into medicine by his physician father, the composer ultimately saw the light and gained immortality with such works as *Symphonie Fantastique* and *Romeo et Juliet.*

38. Count Waldstein. The nobleman often bailed out Beethoven with a loan.

39. The Abraham Lincoln. The ship brings back Pinkerton and his American wife, Kate, to claim his child by Butterfly.

40. Mily Balakirev. Incidentally, he was the only member of "The Five" who had been trained professionally as a musician.

41. Manuel de Falla. When not feeling superstitious, this Spaniard composed *El Amor Brujo* and *Nights in the Gardens of Spain.*

42. Franz Liszt. Having attended an outdoor performance of his son-in-law's *Tristan und Isolde* despite his doctor's warnings, he therefore precipitated his own death.

43. Arnold Schoenberg. He outlived his student and saw Berg's works gather the acclaim that was not present in the composer's lifetime.

44. *Die Walkure.* With her famous horned helmet, she also appears in two other operas of Wagner's Ring cycle: *Siegfried* and *Die Götterdämmerung.*

45. *The Rake's Progress.* Composed in 1950, Stravinsky was inspired by a series of Hogarth drawings.

Mindbenders:

46. Joseph Mathias Hauer. Although Arnold Schöenberg is strongly associated with twelve-tone music, he did not invent it.

47. Victor Hartmann. A friend of Moussorgsky's, the artist died before the music was composed.

48. *Dafne.* This earliest work was followed six years later by *Euridice.*

49. Felix Mendelssohn. The boy delighted the older genius with his own aptitude for composition.

50. Greek. A piece entitled *Pythic Nome,* which described a confrontation between Apollo and a dragon, was composed in 585 B.C.

GEOGRAPHY
AND TRAVEL

Set I:

1. Ninety-five percent of the population of what country are called "Magyars"?

    ?

2. What Moslem republic is known as "The Bengal Nation"?

    ?

3. In which state would you find the Carlsbad Caverns National Park?

    ?

4. What city is the world's largest meat processor?

    ?

5. What nation is considered to be "Joseph Conrad" country?

    ?

6. Where is the largest Gothic structure in the world located?

    ?

7. What is the largest inland sea in the world?

    ?

8. Which state has the highest number of congressional representatives in Washington, D.C.?

    ?

9. Where in North America was the legendary "fountain of youth"?

    ?

10. Who are the fiercely independent people who live on both the French and Spanish sides of the Pyrenees?

    ?

11. What city in India is also the name of a tea?

?

12. Name the capital of Costa Rica.

?

13. In what state would you find Valley Forge State Park?

?

14. What African nation was settled by freed American slaves?

?

15. Name the only other South American country besides Bolivia that does not have a seacoast.

?

Set II:

16. Bohemia is a region in which country?

?

17. Greenland is still ruled by what country?

?

18. The former African state of Rhodesia is now known by what name?

?

19. In which state would you encounter the amusement park, "Dogpatch, U.S.A."?

?

20. What country includes most of the Gobi desert?

?

21. Istanbul was formerly Constantinople, and centuries before that, the city was called by what name?

?

22. If you wished to explore Lapland, to which country would you fly?

?

23. What is the world's highest capital?

?

24. On what island was Saint Paul shipwrecked?

?

25. In what state will you find the National Cowboy Hall of Fame?

?

26. The world-famous Prado Museum is located in the center of what European capital?

?

27. The Quad Cities straddle the border between Iowa and Illinois and consist of Bettendorf, Rock Island, Davenport and what other city?

?

28. In which American city could you stay at the world's tallest hotel?

?

29. Name the highest mountain in Europe.

?

30. Tourists looking for the Great Barrier Reef would travel to what country?

?

Set III:

31. What country has the lowest death rate in Europe?

?

32. In which state could you climb the Sawtooth Mountains?

?

33. In what world capital would you be watching a performance at the Teatro Colon?

?

34. The Belgian Congo is known today by what name?

?

35. Before being absorbed into the U.S.S.R., the Baltic States consisted of Estonia, Lithuania and what other nation?

?

36. What volcanic Greek island was believed to be the site of Atlantis?

?

37. Name the world's largest body of fresh water.

?

38. In what country are the Mayan ruins of Yaxichilan and Tikal?

?

39. In what American city would you locate the longest under-water vehicular tunnel?

?

40. In which state would you visit Okefenokee Swamp Park?

?

41. What nation has three separate capitals?

?

42. The four Imperial Cities of Morocco are Fez, Tangier, Marrakesh and what other city?

?

43. In what country would you find Benares silks?

?

44. What African nation contains the continent's highest mountain?

?

45. What central Pacific island is famous for its bird droppings?

?

Mindbenders:

46. Which state contains the Crater of Diamonds?

?

47. What is the present name of the nation formerly called Bechuanaland?

?

48. In which state would you swim in the Youghiogheny River?

?

49. In which country did the "talking drums" originate?

?

50. In which state will you find "Uncle Sam's House"?

?

Answers

Set I:

1. Hungary. The Magyars are the descendants of the Finno-Ugrian and Asiatic Turkish people.

2. Bangladesh. The nation was created out of the eastern province of Pakistan by a civil war and armed intervention by India.

3. New Mexico. America's most famous underground caverns include over fifty caves and what is known as the Big Room, in which the nation's Capitol could fit with room to spare.

4. Chicago. The city's stockyards have become a tourist attraction.

5. Indonesia. Conrad wrote many stories about this nation of 13,000 separate islands.

6. New York City. Cathedral of St. John the Divine is the largest example of Gothic architecture even though the building has not yet been completed.

7. Caspian Sea. Bordering Iran and the U.S.S.R., this body of water is over 750 miles long and is a source for caviar.

8. California. Having forty-five congressmen for representation, the state is also the nation's most populous with twenty-five million people.

9. Florida. Ponce de Leon came looking for it in 1513 and thought it was in the St. Augustine area.

10. Basques. For centuries, they've fought oppression to maintain their own character, customs and language.

11. Darjeeling. Located on India's northernmost frontier, the town is perched on a 7,000-foot ridge.

12. San Jose. This nation has one of the highest levels of literacy in Latin America.

13. Pennsylvania. Where Washington led his men in 1777, it's probably the most famous military camp in the world.

14. Liberia. The capital of Monrovia was named after U.S. President Monroe.

15. Paraguay. The country relies on tin as its major export.

Set II:

16. Czechoslovakia. After the Treaty of Versailles, the country was formed by joining the three states of Bohemia, Moravia and Slovakia.

17. Denmark. The Danish kingdom also includes the Faeroe Islands between Iceland and Scotland.

18. Zimbabwe. The country achieved independence in 1980.

19. Arkansas. Located near the Ozark National Forest, the park contains all of the famous Al Capp cartoon characters.

20. Mongolia. Bordered by the U.S.S.R. and China, the nation is a huge plateau with the desert in the south.

21. Byzantium. In the early centuries after Christ, it was the center of the opulent Byzantine empire.

22. Finland. After flying to Helsinki, you'd travel north to Rovaniemi, which is where the Lapp culture exists.

23. La Paz. The capital of Bolivia is 12,000 feet above sea level.

24. Malta. It's also considered the historic island for St. John of Jerusalem.

25. Oklahoma. This state also contains the Will Rogers Memorial and Indian City, U.S.A.

26. Madrid. Founded in 1818, the museum contains some of the best paintings of El Greco, Goya, Titian and Hieronymous Bosch.

27. Moline. Davenport is separated from the other three by the Mississippi River.

28. Atlanta. The Peachtree Center Plaza Hotel is 71 stories with a height of 723 feet.

29. Mont Blanc. Measured at 15,771 feet, this mountain is in France and not in Switzerland, which contains most European peaks over thirteen thousand feet.

30. Australia. One of the world's great natural wonders, the reef is just east of the northeast coast of Queensland.

Set III:

31. Iceland. It also boasts the third highest birth rate in Europe.

32. Idaho. These jagged spines in southern Idaho resemble the Alps.

33. Buenos Aires. It is reputed to be the largest opera house in the world.

34. Zaire. The nation's capital, Kinshasha, was formerly known as Leopoldville.

35. Latvia. Its former capital, Riga, was one of the great centers of learning and sophistication in northern Europe.

36. Santorini. Formerly known as Thera, it contains some of the Aegean's most extensive artifacts of ancient Greece.

37. Lake Superior. It's over 383 miles long and 160 miles wide.

38. Guatemala. In some of the temple pyramids, you'll find graffiti over a thousand years old.

39. San Francisco. The BART Trans-Bay Tubes are 3.6 miles in length, connecting the city with Oakland and other East Bay communities.

40. Georgia. Over 60 miles long and 30 miles wide, this swamp is a magnificent wildlife refuge.

41. South Africa. While the legislative branch of government is located in Capetown, the judicial branch is in Bloemfontein, and the administrative branch sits in Pretoria.

42. Rabat. It has also been the nation's capital since 1912.

43. India. Found in the Hindu holy city of Benares, these extraordinary silks are woven with gold.

44. Tanzania. The country contains Mt. Kilimanjaro, which measures 19,340 ft.

45. Nauru. The bird guano which is exported for industrial uses has brought the islanders one of the highest per capita incomes in the world and a ninety-five percent literacy rate!

Mindbenders:

46. Arkansas. It's the only place in the Western Hemisphere where diamonds are found in their natural matrix. Tourists can also dig for the gems.

47. Botswana. The famous Dr. Livingstone settled in the country in the nineteenth century.

48. Pennsylvania. It runs through the rugged Appalachian region.

49. Ghana. The musical instruments are used spiritually and for communication in this nation that was formerly known as the Gold Coast.

50. New Hampshire. Sam Wilson's residence is famous because his markings on his barrels of beef gave rise to the personified symbol of the United States.

HISTORY

Set I:

1. Name the White House Press Secretary who was wounded when Hinckley attempted to assassinate President Reagan.

    ?

2. Of the three ships that accompanied him to America, which one of them actually had Columbus at the helm?

    ?

3. What prompted the resignation of Leopoldo Galtieri as President of Argentina?

    ?

4. What did U.S. Secretary of State William H. Seward buy from Czar Alexander II of Russia?

    ?

5. Why did Spiro Agnew resign from the vice presidency?

    ?

6. Who said, "Genius is one percent inspiration and ninety-nine percent perspiration."

    ?

7. Who killed Alexander Hamilton?

    ?

8. To what area was he referring when General Douglas MacArthur said, "I shall return"?

    ?

9. What was the name of the official Spanish fascist party?

    ?

10. What Indian Chief led the defeat of Custer at the Little Big Horn?

    ?

11. Who was the prosecuting attorney in the Scopes Monkey Trial?

    ?

12. What nation founded the first permanent settlement on the island of Manhattan?

    ?

13. Who became President of the U.S. based on his campaign of "a return to normalcy"?

    ?

14. What American general was known as "Old Blood and Guts"?

    ?

15. Who had the face that launched a thousand ships?

    ?

Set II:

16. What monastic order was in charge of conducting the Spanish Inquisition?

    ?

17. Whom did the Athenians defeat in the Battle of Marathon?

    ?

18. What political group was responsible for the deaths of Austrian Empress Elizabeth, Italian King Umberto I and U.S. President McKinley?

    ?

19. Who said, "Man is born free, and everywhere he is in chains"?

    ?

20. Who was director of the Kaiser Wilhelm Institute of Physics in Berlin from 1914-1933?

    ?

21. Who said, "Remember the Alamo!"

    ?

22. Who was in command of the Allied invasion of North Africa in November, 1942?

    ?

23. Name the very first college to be founded in the United States.

    ?

24. What was the name of the society of British socialists which helped found the Labour Party in 1900?

?

25. Who was the first person to receive *Time* magazine's Man of the Year Award?

?

26. Where was the World War II capital of China?

?

27. Who was the guiding force of the early American Federation of Labor?

?

28. Dag Hammarskjöld was killed in a plane crash while trying to mediate a civil war in what country?

?

29. Who pursued Pancho Villa into Chihuahua, Mexico after Villa and his band killed twenty Americans in New Mexico?

?

30. Robespierre is most closely identified with what execution device?

?

Set III:

31. Who destroyed Solomon's Temple in Jerusalem?

?

32. Which state has been the birthplace of the most U.S. presidents?

?

33. Who was the first democratically elected Marxist president?

?

34. Who said, "Since those whose duty it was to hold the sword of France have let it fall, I have picked up its broken point"?

?

35. Who led the Bay of Pigs invasion?

?

36. Name the acts established by the Federalists in 1798 to silence internal criticism of the government.

?

37. Who was the Missouri slave who initiated a landmark pre–Civil War Supreme Court decision?

?

38. Who organized the communist movement in East Germany and became its first head of state?

?

39. In what war did Winston Churchill work as a war correspondent?

?

40. What Chinese leader was kidnapped by communist sympathizers and later freed by Chou En Lai?

?

41. In what country did Che Gueverra die?

?

42. What was the nickname given to the first German long-range artillery in World War I to blast through French and Belgian defenses?

?

43. Who used in his gubernatorial campaign the slogan, "Every man a king!"?

?

44. Who built the Great Wall of China?

?

45. Name the monarch who united all the Scandinavian countries under one rule?

?

Mindbenders:

46. Who was Muckle John?

?

47. Before he committed suicide, whom did Hitler appoint as President of the German Reich?

?

48. Who made the first nonstop transatlantic flight?

?

49. In which war did the Charge of the Light Brigade occur?

?

50. What Queen of England never set foot on English soil?

?

Answers

Set I:

1. James Brady. He was shot in the head and is still partially disabled.

2. Santa Maria. Spain subsequently made him an admiral and Governor General of all new lands. He died, however, in obscurity and neglect.

3. Loss of the Falklands. It was alleged that he went to war with England to protect his regime from falling.

4. Alaska. The 1867 purchase became known as "Seward's Folly."

5. Income tax evasion. It occurred while Agnew was Governor of Maryland, and Gerald Ford replaced him as vice president on October 12, 1973.

6. Thomas Edison. Besides inventing the first practical electric light, he also patented a record player and a carbon microphone.

7. Aaron Burr. Although he served as vice president under Jefferson, Burr's political career ended after he shot Hamilton in a duel in 1804.

8. Corregidor. He did return to that part of the Philippines two and a half years later on October 20, 1944.

9. Falange. It was the only party permitted under Franco and was founded in 1933 by Jose Antonio Primo de Rivera.

10. Sitting Bull. Leader of the Prairie Sioux, they killed Custer and over 200 of his men at this historic battle in 1876.

11. William Jennings Bryan. He faced defense attorney Clarence Darrow in the 1925 trial over the teaching of evolution in Dayton, Tennessee.

12. Netherlands. The Dutch West India Company established the settlement in 1623.

13. Warren Harding. Ironically, his administration was plagued by corruption and the infamous "Teapot Dome" scandal.

14. George Patton, Jr. Coming from a long line of military leaders and statesmen, he led the Third Army after the D-Day invasion in June, 1944.

15. Helen of Troy. After she ran off with Paris of Troy, her desperate husband, Menelaus, rallied the Greeks to wage the Trojan War.

Set II:

16. Dominicans. Under a papal order of Innocent III, they routed out supposed heretics and burned them at the stake.

17. Persians. The Greeks fought well since the Persians outnumbered them by ten to one!

18. Anarchists. Originally a peaceful movement of idealists typified by Leo Tolstoy, the group turned violent around the turn of the century.

19. Jean Jacques Rousseau. Written in 1762 in his *Social Contract,* his philosophy had a profound effect on Goethe as well as on the French revolutionists.

20. Albert Einstein. He fled to the U.S. to escape antisemitism.

21. Colonel Sidney Sherman. A month and a half after he killed everyone in the Alamo, Santa Anna was captured at the Battle of San Jacinto.

22. Eisenhower. When elected President in 1953, he became the first army president since Ulysses S. Grant.

23. Harvard. The college was founded October 28, 1636, in the same year that compulsory education was established in Boston.

24. Fabians. An articulate member of this group was George Bernard Shaw.

25. Charles Lindbergh. The award was inaugurated in 1927.

26. Chungking. The 1937 Japanese invasion of northern China forced Chiang Kai-Shek to relocate the capital from Peking to Chungking until the end of the war.

27. Samuel Gompers. He was a New York cigarmaker who was the president of the A.F. of L. from 1886 until his death in 1924.

28. Congo. Having served as Secretary General for the U.N., he was awarded a posthumous Nobel Peace Prize in 1961.

29. General John Pershing. He crossed the Rio Grande with 6,000 troops but never found Villa.

30. Guillotine. During the "Reign of Terror" from 1793 to 1795, he and the Jacobins executed thousands of French noblemen, priests and their opponents.

Set III:

31. Nebuchadnezzar II. Although demolished by this Babylonian monarch, the Jewish temple was rebuilt when the Persians conquered Babylon and freed the Jews.

32. Virginia. Numbering as illustrious sons of Virginia were: Washington, Jefferson, Madison, Monroe, Harrison, Tyler, Taylor and Wilson.

33. Salvador Allende. This Chilean leader died in the 1973 overthrow by CIA-backed General Augusto Pinochet.

34. Charles de Gaulle. Heading the French government for eleven years, he settled the problem of Algerian independence, strengthened France's atomic potential and withdrew from NATO.

35. Jose Cardona. He led a group of Cuban exiles in an attempt to overthrow Castro.

36. Alien and Sedition Acts. They were passed in an atmosphere of growing world conservatism following the excesses of the French Revolution.

37. Dred Scott. The 1857 decision affirmed the right of slaves to own property.

38. Walther Ulbricht. He led the Socialist Unity Party from 1946 to 1971.

39. Boer War. Fought from 1899 until 1902, the war established British sovereignty over the Afrikaans.

40. Chiang Kai-shek. He was President of China from 1928 until the Communists took over in 1949.

41. Bolivia. He was executed by Bolivian soldiers after attempting to start an insurrection of Bolivian peasants using guerilla warfare.

42. Big Bertha. These giant cannons could hit targets seventy-six miles away.

43. Huey Long. Known as "The Kingfish," this Louisiana governor promoted his share-the-wealth plan guaranteeing every family a minimum annual income of $5,000. He was assassinated in 1935 by the son of one of his opponents.

44. Emperor Shih Huang Ti. Built between 221 and 210 B.C., this man-made marvel was erected to keep out the Tartars.

45. Queen Margrethe I of Denmark. The Scandinavian union dissolved in 1523 when Sweden became independent and by

1616, the Swedes were the greatest Protestant power in
Europe.

Mindbenders:

46. Fool of England. Under the reign of Charles I, he became
the last official Fool of England.

47. Karl Doenitz. This German Grand Admiral headed the
Reich from May 1 to May 23, 1945.

48. John Alcock and Arthur W. Brown. These British World
War I pilots flew from Newfoundland to Ireland in 1919.
Lindbergh made the first *solo* nonstop flight in 1927 from
New York to Paris.

49. Crimean War. Lasting from 1853 till 1856, Turkey, Britain
and France allied against Russia.

50. Queen Berengaria of Navarre. Marrying King Richard the
Lion-Hearted in Cyprus, she returned to France to await his
return from the Crusades, but he never came back.

LANGUAGE AND LITERATURE

Set I:

1. What is Romeo's family name?
   ?
2. Who's the hero of Dorothy L. Sayer's detective novels?
   ?
3. During Thoreau's stay at Walden Pond, he spent one night in jail for what crime?
   ?
4. Who wrote about the Joad family and their trip to California to pick fruit?
   ?
5. Leopold Bloom had a busy day on June 16, 1904 in what city?
   ?
6. How did Ernest Hemingway die?
   ?
7. Who is Scotland's national poet?
   ?
8. In what language was Dante's *Divine Comedy* written?
   ?
9. At the end of Fitzgerald's *The Great Gatsby,* where was Jay Gatsby buried?
   ?
10. How many marriages did Scarlett O'Hara have before she met her match in Rhett Butler?
    ?
11. What's the family name of Peter Pan's young friends?
    ?

12. Name the alphabet used to write Russian.

    ?

13. Who wrote the best-selling novel about a group of rabbits on a life-or-death trip to find a new home?

    ?

14. Where did Alice go after she'd seen Wonderland?

    ?

15. Which author created a cult after publishing a book entitled, *The Hobbit*?

    ?

Set II:

16. What's the archaic name used to call the boy who helps out around a printing press?

    ?

17. In what novel do a couple of "baddiwad droogs drast and crack some lewdies they viddy and have horroshow time"?

    ?

18. In *Women in Love,* what is D.H. Lawrence's resolution to the battle of the sexes?

    ?

19. Peter De Vries's satiric novel, *I Hear America Swinging,* begins with a parody of what American poet?

    ?

20. What Greek tragedian earned the epithet "father of tragedy"?

    ?

21. What was the title of Charlotte Brontë's sister's only novel?

    ?

22. What early English poet never completed his masterpiece of stories told during a pilgrimage?

    ?

23. Frontier hero, Natty Bumppo, appears in what group of stories by James Fenimore Cooper?

    ?

24. While working as a reporter in New York, which author published his first novel, *Maggie: A Girl of the Streets,* under a pseudonym?

    ?

25. Of what philosophical movement was Ralph Waldo Emerson the central figure?

?

26. What was the name of the town Faulkner modeled after his home town of Oxford, Mississippi in his novels?

?

27. Fuzzy-Wuzzy, Mandalay and Gunga Din are all found in what body of verse?

?

28. Sinclair Lewis's *Main Street* takes place in what fictional town?

?

29. When Charlotte wrote the words, "Some pig!", to what character was she referring?

?

30. In Ken Kesey's novel, *One Flew Over the Cuckoo's Nest,* what is the name of the patient who threatens Nurse Ratched's hold over the ward?

?

Set III:

31. In what county live the Compson family with their cook, Dilsey?

?

32. What is the first prize in Shirley Jackson's "The Lottery"?

?

33. What court permitted James Joyce's *Ulysses* to enter the United States after it was called obscene?

?

34. What is the title of John Updike's first play and first "historical" work about the only Pennsylvanian to reach the White House?

?

35. Name the Greek tragedian who, unlike Euripides, never placed third in the dramatic competitions and only very rarely came in second.

?

36. Under what pseudonym did Colette and Henri Gauthier-

Villars co-write the four *Claudine* novels between 1900 and 1903?

?

37. What is the title of Aristophanes' play concerning the women's sex strike against war?

?

38. What work by Charles Dickens was first serialized?

?

39. To what audience was Fielding's *Tom Jones* addressed?

?

40. Who killed Dorian Gray?

?

41. What was the name of Christopher Robin's father?

?

42. What Irish author chose his permanent residence based on the record of longevity he found in the local graveyard?

?

43. Where is "The Poet's Corner"?

?

44. The relatively new word "astronaut" uses two word parts from what language?

?

45. Where was the man headed when he was buttonholed by the rather long-winded Ancient Mariner?

?

Mindbenders:

46. What Irish playwright wrote a controversial, riot-provoking work about the Easter Rebellion?

?

47. Who gave King Arthur his Round Table?

?

48. Along with Robert Southey, which poet developed pantisocracy—a plan for a utopian community on the Susquehanna River in Pennsylvania?

?

49. After 1862, in what color of clothing did Emily Dickinson choose to dress?

?

50. Who was the first author to decline the Nobel Prize for Literature?

?

Answers

Set I:

1. Montague. Juliet's family name was Capulet.

2. Lord Peter Wimsey. He was an aristocratic sleuth of enormous wit and charm.

3. Refusing to pay his poll tax. Thoreau went to Walden Pond to seek answers for "the mass of men [who] lead lives of quiet desperation."

4. John Steinbeck. They were the subject of his 1939 novel, *The Grapes of Wrath* which won him a Pulitzer Prize.

5. Dublin. Bloom is the principal player in the intricate maze of Joyce's *Ulysses*.

6. Suicide. Realizing his cancer was incurable, he shot himself near his home in Idaho.

7. Robert Burns. Besides his volumes of verse, he also authored "Auld Lang Syne."

8. Italian. Prior to *La Divina Commedia* which was written between 1307 and 1321, literature was written primarily in Latin.

9. Long Island. The author's full name was Francis Scott Key Fitzgerald.

10. Two. She was widowed twice.

11. Darling. J.M. Barrie's work was written in 1904.

12. Cyrillic. It was named after its inventor, Saint Cyril, who lived in the ninth century A.D.

13. Richard Adams. The novel was entitled *Watership Down*.

14. *Through the Looking-Glass*. Charles Lutwidge Dodgson, using the pseudonym of Lewis Carroll, wrote this sequel in 1872.

15. J.R.R. Tolkien. After this work was published in 1937, this Oxford professor began writing his magnificent trilogy, *The Lord of the Rings*.

Set II:

16. Printer's devil. The occupation was so named because in an earlier time, the lad would be black with splattered ink.

17. *Clockwork Orange*. Author Anthony Burgess created a frightening Anglo-Russian patois for this novel.

18. Marriage or death. In the book, Birkin and Ursula get married, whereas Gerald dies, to Gudrun's dismay.

19. Walt Whitman. Undoubtedly, De Vries was inspired by Whitman's celebration of sexuality in his *Leaves of Grass*.

20. Aeschylus. His are the earliest surviving specimens of the art; also, he is virtually the creator of the medium in which he worked.

21. *Wuthering Heights*. Written by Emily Brontë, the novel was published in 1847 after Charlotte's *Jane Eyre,* which was more popular.

22. Chaucer. In his *Canterbury Tales,* the pilgrims were heading to the shrine of St. Thomas à Becket in the English cathedral town.

23. *The Leatherstocking Tales*. The final book in which Natty appeared was *The Deerslayer,* written in 1841.

24. Stephen Crane. He's credited with introducing realism into the American novel with this grim and unpopular first work.

25. Transcendentalism. He stated the movement's main principle in his work, *Nature* which stressed the mystical unity of nature.

26. Jefferson. Faulkner was awarded the Nobel Prize for Literature in 1949.

27. *Barrack Room Ballads*. Rudyard Kipling wrote them to celebrate the English soldier who was posted abroad.

28. Gopher Prairie. It's likely that Lewis based this fictional town on his own birthplace of Sauk Centre, Minnesota.

29. Wilbur. This is the name that E.B. White gave to the hero-pig in his book, *Charlotte's Web*.

30. Randle Patrick McMurphy. He leads the revolt with the likes of Ruckly, Colonel Matterson, Martini and the Chief.

Set III:

31. Yoknapatawpha County. Faulkner set many of his stories here, including *The Sound and the Fury* and *As I Lay Dying*.

32. Death by stoning. This is the chilling revelation that comes late in this great American short story.

33. United States District Court of New York. The Honorable John M. Woolsey rendered the landmark decision on December 6, 1933, in which he commented: "In respect of the recurrent emergence of the theme of sex in the minds of his characters, it must always be remembered that his locale was Celtic and his season Spring."

34. *Buchanan Dying*. It deals with the life and death of James Buchanan, Lincoln's immediate predecessor.

35. Sophocles. His first victory over Aeschylus in the competitions was in 468 B.C.

36. "Willy." It's said that Gauthier-Villars, Colette's first husband, would keep her locked in a room until she finished writing that day's required number of pages.

37. *Lysistrata.* This biting satire is one of the first examples of antiwar propaganda.

38. *Sketches by Boz.* This 1836 work was popular in London's Old Monthly Magazine.

39. Common men. This novel carried on the tradition of Fielding's earlier *Joseph Andrews* and *Jonathan Wild,* which spoke to those "who partake of the more amiable weaknesses of human nature."

40. It was suicide. In Oscar Wilde's novel, Gray stabs the horrifying portrait of himself and is found dead with a knife in the heart.

41. A.A. Milne. The author used his son's name as a central character in the "Pooh" stories.

42. G.B. Shaw. He savored and heavily promoted his own eccentric reputation.

43. Westminster Abbey. The south end of the south transept contains tombs or monuments to Chaucer, Spenser, Drayton, Ben Jonson, Milton, Shakespeare and a host of others.

44. Greek. The roots can be found in such words as *astronomy* and *nautical.*

45. A wedding. In Coleridge's doleful poem, the man chafes at being kept from the ceremony.

Mindbenders:

46. Sean O'Casey. Interestingly, this native of Dublin was plagued by poor eyesight and couldn't read until he was twelve.

47. King Leodegrance. He was Guinevere's father and gave the table to the couple when they were married.

48. Coleridge. The ideal community failed for having a lack of funds.

49. White. Only seven of her one thousand poems were published during her lifetime.

50. Boris Pasternak. The Soviet government pressured him to turn down the prize in 1958. The only other author to decline this award was Jean Paul Sartre in 1964.

THEATER AND DANCE

Set I:

1. What child actress played the Broadway and ultimately the movie lead in *The Bad Seed*?

    ?

2. Broadway's first Auntie Mame was played by what well-known film actress?

    ?

3. Who is Nina—the word that shows up in all the drawings by theater cartoonist Al Hirschfeld?

    ?

4. The director, Jose Quintero, is most closely associated with the works of what playwright?

    ?

5. Before his exile from Germany, Kurt Weill collaborated with Bertolt Brecht on what musical play?

    ?

6. *Six Characters in Search of an Author* was written by which playwright?

    ?

7. Name the Broadway impresario who was connected to Anna Held, Billie Burke and Fanny Brice.

    ?

8. Who was the ballerina who studied with Ruth St. Denis and Ted Shawn and left to found one of the great modern dance companies in America?

    ?

9. In what city did John Barrymore begin his stage career?

    ?

125

10. Which American dancer opened a school for dance in Moscow in 1921 at the invitation of the Soviet government?

?

11. Name the musical in which the Marx Brothers first appeared on Broadway?

?

12. What was the dance that was immortalized by Jacques Offenbach in Paris in the late nineteenth century?

?

13. Which singer started her career playing comic fat girl parts on Broadway and finally had a radio career that lasted nearly fifty years?

?

14. What was George Balanchine's native country?

?

15. Clifford Odets's *Golden Boy* was a play written about what sport?

?

Set II:

16. The standard, "Bewitched, Bothered and Bewildered," was written for which Rogers and Hart musical?

?

17. The "mambo" was introduced to the United States from what country?

?

18. What currently successful screen and television writer co-wrote the book for *A Funny Thing Happened on the Way to the Forum*?

?

19. In the original Broadway production of *Equus*, psychiatrist Martin Dysart was played by what eminent actor?

?

20. What is the name of the unseen but ever present lead in Mary Chase's hilarious play?

?

21. Who founded the first all-black ballet company in America?

?

22. Name the innovative Elizabethan set designer whose ideas survive to today.

?

23. *Please Don't Eat the Daisies* was a comic look at the life of what well-known theater critic?

?

24. What's the name of the dance festival that's been held in New England every summer for decades?

?

25. In the original Broadway production of *Arsenic and Old Lace,* the homicidal maniac character, Jonathan Brewster, was played by what actor?

?

26. Who wrote the music for the Broadway hit, *DuBarry Was a Lady*?

?

27. In Tennessee Williams's original production of *Cat on a Hot Tin Roof,* the pivotal role of Maggie the Cat was played by what actress?

?

28. Name the modern play that is produced more than any other in American high school productions.

?

29. Which of Eugene O'Neill's plays was based on a fifth-century B.C. Greek tragedy?

?

30. What is the world's largest indoor theatre?

?

Set III:

31. Who wrote the book for *Bye, Bye Birdie, Carnival* and *Hello Dolly*?

?

32. The Rodgers and Hammerstein musical, *Carousel,* was based on what European play?

?

33. Name the system of dance movement developed by the Viennese-born musician, Jacques Dalcroze.

?

34. Early French dramatist Jean Baptiste Poquelin became immortalized by what other name?

?

35. What was the name of the first Broadway play in which Henry Fonda performed?

?

36. What world-famous comic performer started his stage career at the age of fourteen as a pantomime juggler?

?

37. Aaron Copland wrote the music and Martha Graham choreographed what classic modern ballet?

?

38. Samuel Beckett's "Waiting For Godot" was originally written for the stage in what language?

?

39. Which world-famous playwright was also a medical doctor?

?

40. What dance step introduced initially at Harlem's Apollo Theater became the rival of the Charleston?

?

41. In the original Broadway production of *I Remember Mama,* the character of Nels was played by what actor?

?

42. Name the Broadway director who established a repertory theatre in the Midwest.

?

43. Besides her recent one-woman show, Lena Horne's only other starring Broadway role was in what musical?

?

44. T.S. Eliot's *Murder in the Cathedral* was based on the death of what historical figure?

?

45. Name the Broadway musical hit of 1942 which featured an all-soldier cast.

?

Mindbenders:

46. Who invented the theater staple known as grease paint?

?

47. What 1941 play caused the archbishops of Paris to warn all

Roman Catholics not to attend and threatened excommunication to those who did?

?

48. Name the ballet in which Edith Sitwell read her poetry.

?

49. What was the play written by Chinese playwright, Tsas Y, which was perceived as an attack on the traditional family system?

?

50. Name the Broadway musical which included among its band members Benny Goodman, Glenn Miller and Jimmy Dorsey.

?

Answers

Set I:

1. Patty McCormack. Playing the eight-year-old murderer, Rhoda, in Maxwell Anderson's melodrama, she committed four grisly murders—one of which included her mother.

2. Rosalind Russell. She went on to star in the film and was joined by her Broadway co-star, Peggy Cass.

3. His daughter. He started hiding her name in his drawings, including the number of times it was used. Now counting "Ninas" has become such a popular game that he can't stop the practice.

4. Eugene O'Neill. Cofounding New York's Circle in the Square Theater, Quintero has dedicated himself to directing and coproducing O'Neill's major plays.

5. *The Threepenny Opera.* In 1928, they based this mordant musical on the eighteenth-century comedy *The Beggar's Opera.*

6. Luigi Pirandello. Italy's major modern playwright wrote this

THE TRIVIA CHALLENGE

play as a result of dreams he had after committing his wife to an insane asylum in 1918.

7. Florenz Ziegfeld. While they were all Follies stars, Burke and Held were married to the celebrated producer.

8. Martha Graham. She made her first New York solo performance in 1926 at the age of thirty-one.

9. New York City. Barrymore was twenty-one and appeared in *Glad of It* by Clyde Fitch.

10. Isadora Duncan. While there, she met and married a Russian poet although neither of them could speak the other's language.

11. *The Coconuts.* It opened at New York's Lyric Theater in 1925.

12. Cancan. It was introduced in his comic opera, *Orpheus in the Underworld.*

13. Kate Smith. She first sang Irving Berlin's "God Bless America" in a 1938 Armistice Day radio broadcast.

14. Russia. While on tour with the Soviet State Dancers, he defected in Paris, changed his name and joined the Ballet Russe de Monte Carlo.

15. Boxing. John Garfield, Lee J. Cobb, Karl Malden and Elia Kazan were among the original New York cast.

Set II:

16. *Pal Joey.* Said to be the first musical using moral realism, it was adapted from a John O'Hara book and was Gene Kelly's first starring role on Broadway.

17. Cuba. Arriving in 1950, it became a dance craze and is now a standard Latin dance step.

18. Larry Gelbart. Besides developing the TV series, "M*A*S*H," he also cowrote the film *Tootsie*.

19. Anthony Hopkins. Peter Firth played the boy in the Peter Shaffer play when it was first mounted on Broadway in 1974.

20. *Harvey.* He was a six-foot-tall white rabbit—called a pooka —that could only be seen by the character, Elwood P. Dowd.

21. Arthur Mitchell. After starring for many years in Balanchine's New York City Ballet, he founded the now-famous Dance Theater of Harlem.

22. Inigo Jones. He won fame for his fantastic spectacles of moving sets and unusual lighting.

23. Walter Kerr. Written by his wife, Jean, the play exposed the critic's personal foibles, affectations and frustrations.

24. Jacob's Pillow. The festival was founded by Ted Shawn in the Berkshires.

25. Boris Karloff. Raymond Massey played the part in the film version.

26. Cole Porter. He also wrote the lyrics. Starring Ethel Merman and Bert Lahr, the show's big number was "Friendship."

27. Barbara Bel Geddes. Staged in 1955, *Cat* starred her with Ben Gazzara, Burl Ives and Mildred Dunnock.

28. *You Can't Take It with You.* This 1936 Kaufman and Hart comedy first starred Josephine Hull and George Tobias.

29. *Mourning Becomes Electra.* It opened in 1931 at the New York Guild Theater with Alla Nazimova and Alice Brady in leading roles.

30. Radio City Music Hall. Opened in December 1932, it is one of America's best examples of the Art Deco style.

Set III:

31. Michael Stewart. His first three Broadway musicals had record-breaking runs of over 400 performances.

32. Liliom. Written by Hungarian playwright, Ferenc Molnar, the dramatic play heralded Ingrid Bergman's Broadway debut in 1940 co-starring with Burgess Meredith and Elia Kazan.

33. Eurythmics. He designed it as a communication between brain and body with the help of rhythm.

34. Molière. After founding the *Comédie Française,* he was often ridiculed for his scathing comedic attacks on hypocrisy, causing Louis XIV to often intercede for him.

35. *The Game of Love and Death.* Fonda was twenty-four years old, and it was almost twenty years before his most famous Broadway role in 1948's *Mister Roberts.*

36. W.C. Fields. Performing for England's Edward VII in 1901, this gentleman's real name was William Clark Dukenfield.

37. *Appalachian Spring.* This American classic was premiered in Washington, D.C.

38. French. Opening in Paris in 1953 as *En Attendant Godot,* the highly acclaimed play was translated by Beckett, an Irish expatriate living in France, into English.

39. Anton Chekhov. He said, "Medicine is my wife and literature is my mistress."

40. Black Bottom. It later was introduced on Broadway in George White's *Scandals.*

41. Marlon Brando. It was produced by Rodgers and Hammerstein, and the playbill noted that Brando was born in Calcutta where his father was engaged in geological research.

42. Tyrone Guthrie. The Guthrie Theater in Minneapolis was established in 1959 and is world famous.

43. *Jamaica.* Beginning her career in Harlem's Cotton Club, she spent most of her career in Hollywood. In this show, she introduced the song, "Coconut Sweet."

44. Thomas à Becket. The Archbishop of Canterbury was assassinated in his church in 1170.

45. *This Is the Army.* The show had music and lyrics by Irving Berlin.

Mindbenders:

46. Ludwig Leichner. This German singer developed the formula in 1865 and sold them in different colors and liners. Today's stage makeup is much the same as his original formula.

47. *The Martyrdom of St. Sebastian.* It was written by Gabriele D'Annunzio and had music by Debussy. D'Annunzio's works had been placed on the index of forbidden books by the church just two weeks before this play opened.

48. *Facade.* It was first performed in 1923 in London with music by composer Howard Walton.

49. *Thunderstorm.* It was written in the style of a Greek tragedy.

50. *Strike Up the Band.* It played at New York's Times Square Theater in 1930.

POP MUSIC

Set I:

1. In what city would you have found the "Cavern Club"?
   ?
2. What was Elvis Presley's first record label?
   ?
3. Who originated the "Wall of Sound"?
   ?
4. What singing group originally called themselves "The Primes"?
   ?
5. Who sang "I'm Sorry"?
   ?
6. What was the title of Elvis Presley's first film?
   ?
7. Who ran the "Caravan of Stars"?
   ?
8. What city was known as "Hitsville, U.S.A."?
   ?
9. Which notorious rock star's father was an admiral in the United States Navy?
   ?
10. Who wrote the hit song, "My Guy"?
    ?
11. What American female disco singer got her start in Germany?
    ?

12. What famous female vocalist once sang with a group called "The Stone Poneys"?

?

13. Who sang "Society's Child"?

?

14. What artist owns Rocket Records?

?

15. What country superstar once served time in San Quentin?

?

Set II:

16. Who played the national anthem which closed the Woodstock Festival?

?

17. From what cult did the group "Kiss" get its name?

?

18. Who wrote the pop song with the longest title in the history of rock?

?

19. What other act was on the same bill with the Beatles at Brooklyn's Paramount Theater in 1964?

?

20. Who sang "I Love You Ringo"?

?

21. Considered a milestone in rock history, what was the Moondog Ball?

?

22. What is considered the first of the folk-rock songs?

?

23. What group was noted for the "Tottenham Sound"?

?

24. What was the very first song to receive a gold record?

?

25. Who was billed under the name "Derek" as part of the group, "Derek and the Dominoes"?

?

26. What was the name of Phil Spector's record label?

?

27. Who sang lead for "Paul Revere and the Raiders"?

?

28. What lead singer was once married to actress Faye Dunaway?

?

29. Who sang "The Battle of New Orleans" and was tragically killed shortly after the recording was made?

?

30. Which Beatle was the first to record a solo album?

?

Set III:

31. What was Brian Epstein's occupation when he first met the Beatles?

?

32. What was the very first rock song ever used in a film?

?

33. What is the oldest surviving pop singing group?

?

34. According to the song, "American Pie," what was the day that the music died?

?

35. What was the first group to appear on "American Bandstand" when it went on national television?

?

36. What singer acquired the reputation as "queen of the weepers"?

?

37. Who was on the first cover of *Rolling Stone* magazine?

?

38. Who sings on the album, "Best of the Beatles"?

?

39. Where did the group, "Buffalo Springfield," get its name?

?

40. What was the first rock song to get on the Billboard charts?

?

41. Which of the Drifters' songs was the only one to hit number one?

?

42. Who played lead guitar on the Beach Boys' "Good Vibrations"?

?

43. Who has had the most number-one records?

?

44. What group of musicians met in art school?

?

45. Who is considered the grandfather of punk rock?

?

Mindbenders:

46. With whom did John Lennon make his last live appearance?

?

47. What singing duo was once known as "Tom and Jerry"?

?

48. Who was the original host of "American Bandstand" on television?

?

49. On what show did Elvis Presley make his national television debut?

?

50. What Pulitzer Prize–winning playwright cowrote a hit song?

?

Answers

Set I:

1. Liverpool. This nightspot was where the Beatles got their start.

2. Sun Records. They subsequently sold his contract to RCA for a paltry $35,000.

3. Phil Spector. His first million-record seller was "To Know Him Is to Love Him."

4. The Temptations. They often sang at local Detroit high

school dances with another group called the Primettes—who later became The Supremes.

5. Brenda Lee. She was known as "Little Miss Dynamite"— the little girl with the great big voice.

6. *Love Me Tender*. Paramount signed him to a three-picture deal five days after he screen-tested for them in 1956.

7. Dick Clark. Teenagers across the country paid $1.50 to see a live, four-hour rock show. The first caravan included a newly formed group, The Supremes.

8. Detroit. It was the birthplace of Motown Records, at 2648 West Grand Avenue in the motor city.

9. Jim Morrison. He often tried to deny this fact about his dad's profession.

10. Smokey Robinson. He still performs today and is vice president with Motown, where he writes his songs.

11. Donna Summer. While appearing in the German production of *Hair* she met composer, Giorgio Moroder.

12. Linda Ronstadt. In 1968 they recorded the hit song, "Different Drum" which was written by *future* Monkee, Michael Nesmith.

13. Janis Ian. Although not autobiographical according to Ian, she wrote the song when she was just 14 years old, in 1967.

14. Elton John. He formed the company in 1973 but didn't record for them until 1976 when his prior contract with DJM expired.

15. Merle Haggard. While serving time there, he saw Johnny Cash give his now-famous performance.

Set II:

16. Jimi Hendrix. He was considered by many to be the best guitarist in rock and roll.

17. Satanism. It actually stands for: *K*nights *I*n the *S*ervice of *S*atan.

18. Ray Stevens. The song was, "Jeremiah Peabody's Polyunsaturated Quick-Dissolving Fast-Acting Pleasant-Tasting Green and Purple Pills."

19. Steve Lawrence and Eydie Gorme. Although thought to be the weirdest rock bill in history because the Beatles shared the bill with Steve and Eydie, historians forget that Steve Lawrence was on top of the charts then with "Go Away Little Girl."

20. Bonnie Jo Mason. This was the name used by Cher long before she met Sonny Bono.

21. First rock concert. Sponsored by Alan Freed in Cleveland in 1952, this concert attracted 20,000 people while there was only seating for a capacity crowd of 3,000.

22. "Mr. Tambourine Man." It was recorded by the Byrds in 1965 who, in those days, were called America's answer to the Beatles.

23. The Dave Clark Five. They were the Beatles' archrivals during the early days of the "British Invasion."

24. "Catch a Falling Star." This Perry Como hit received the first gold record ever given by the Recording Industry Association of America, in 1958.

25. Eric Clapton. Their biggest hit was "Layla" in 1972. It was the nickname for George Harrison's wife, who later married Clapton.

26. Philles. It derived its name from the first names of its two founders, *Phil* Spector and *Les* Sills—and not from the city of Philadelphia.

139

27. Mark Lindsay. The Raiders were the first rock group ever signed by the then-rather-staid Columbia Records label.

28. Peter Wolf. He was the lead singer with the J. Geils Band.

29. Johnny Horton. He was killed in a car crash before his recording went on to become the number one song of 1960.

30. George Harrison. He did the soundtrack album for the 1968 film, *Wonderwall*.

Set III:

31. Selling records. He worked in his family's shop.

32. "Rock Around the Clock." It was used in the opening of the film, *Blackboard Jungle,* in 1955.

33. The Four Tops. They have stayed together intact since 1953.

34. February 3, 1959. It was the day the plane crashed killing Buddy Holly, Richie Valens and The Big Bopper.

35. The Chordettes. They were responsible for such hits as, "Mr. Sandman," "Eddie My Love," and "Lollipop."

36. Leslie Gore. Her major hits included "It's My Party," "Judy's Turn to Cry," and "You Don't Own Me."

37. John Lennon. It first appeared on the newsstands in 1967.

38. Peter Best. Ringo was brought in to replace Best as the drummer for the Beatles. In order to cash in on their later success, Best recorded his own album, "Best of the Beatles."

39. From a steamroller. It was parked across the street from the studio where the now-legendary group used to rehearse.

40. "Crazy Man Crazy." Some claim that this 1953 Bill Haley hit is the first rock and roll song because of this status, but many historians claim other songs came first.

41. "Save the Last Dance for Me." It was recorded in 1960 when Ben E. King was singing lead.

42. Glen Campbell. He replaced Brian Wilson, who was in temporary retirement.

43. The Supremes. They produced twelve number-one hits between 1964 and 1969.

44. The Talking Heads. Chris Franz, Tina Weymouth and David Byrne went to the Rhode Island School of Design. Jerry Harrison, unfortunately, only went to Harvard.

45. Iggy Pop. He began his bizarre stage theatrics as Iggy and the Stooges in 1968.

Mindbenders:

46. Elton John. When Lennon allowed Elton John to record "Lucy in the Sky with Diamonds," he agreed to appear on stage live if it hit number one; when it did, in 1974, Lennon joined Elton John on stage at a New York City concert.

47. Simon and Garfunkel. They were still in high school and sang the 1957 hit song "Hey School Girl."

48. Bob Horn. He hosted the show for the first three years. When he was arrested for drunk driving, Dick Clark, who was already doing the show on radio, was brought in to replace him.

49. The Dorsey Brothers. He appeared on their show nine months before he made the first of his now-famous Ed Sullivan appearances.

50. William Saroyan. He cowrote the 1951 hit "Come On-A My House" for Rosemary Clooney.

THE INQUISITION

(The following contains questions from every subject category in the book. The questions should make the previous "mindbenders" seem easy in comparison.)

1. Name the painting that most art historians believe changed the course of twentieth-century art.
   ?
2. In the world of plants, what is an epiphyte?
   ?
3. Who sang the demo record for Brenda Lee's 1961 pop hit "Fool Number One"?
   ?
4. If you ordered "Fricandeau" in a fine restaurant, what would you be served?
   ?
5. What is near Castle Rock, South Dakota?
   ?
6. What did Peter Hodgson invent?
   ?
7. What was the name of the first animal sent into space?
   ?
8. Who founded the Civic Repertory Theatre?
   ?
9. From the pages of ancient history, who was Incitatus?
   ?
10. What symptom occurs when you have the disorder known as "psilosis"?
    ?
11. Who wrote the novel *Liza of Lambeth*?
    ?
12. On that fateful day in 1929 when the New York Stock

Exchange collapsed, what was the price of General Motors when the market opened?

?

13. In an immortal western film, what was the name of the Marshall of Hadleyville?

?

14. What classical composer invented the phrase "Back to Bach"?

?

15. According to the Bible, what is east of Eden?

?

16. What racetrack was the first to have a photo finish?

?

17. What famous radio program had the theme song "How Can I Leave You"?

?

18. Which major-league baseball player had this century's single-season highest batting average?

?

19. The kangaroo is an excellent example of what family of animals?

?

20. What medieval clergyman is considered to be the father of Gothic architecture?

?

21. The lines "I am a sick man. I am a spiteful man." launch what famous short story?

?

22. What vocal group did Kim Carnes sing with in the 1960s?

?

23. F. Scott Fitzgerald and Ernest Hemingway met for the first time at what Parisian bar?

?

24. In a famous 1965 Academy Award–nominated film, what was the profession of the character named Sol Nazerman?

?

25. What part of the body is known as the sacrum?

?

26. From a famous 1950s television series, which actor played the character Milton Armitage?

?

27. What American university has the largest football stadium?

?

28. What artistic accomplishment occurred on the U.S.S. *Minden*?

?

29. In Voltaire's classic novel, what was the name of Candide's trusting servant?

?

30. Name the rainiest spot in the United States.

?

Answers

1. "Les Demoiselles d'Avignon." Painted by Pablo Picasso, the work introduced cubism.

2. Air plant. This plant may grow on another, but it's not parasitic.

3. Loretta Lynn. She was unknown then, and the record was turned down by both Columbia and Capitol before Decca picked it up.

4. Larded veal. It is glazed and roasted in its own juices.

5. The exact geographic center of the *fifty* United States.

6. Silly Putty. It was the rage of the 1950s.

7. Ham (acronym for Hollowman Aerospace Medical Center). He was a chimpanzee who was launched into space on January 31, 1961.

8. Eva Le Gallienne. She founded the theatre in 1926, becoming one of the first actresses to have her own repertory company.

9. Caligula's favorite horse. The emperor named him a consul of Rome.

10. Your hair falls out.

11. W. Somerset Maugham. Having written this first novel in 1897, Maugham had to wait eighteen years until the publication of his first successful novel, *Of Human Bondage*.

12. 60¾. Two orders for twenty-thousand-share blocks of General Motors and Kennecott Copper set in motion the ultimate collapse.

13. Will Kane. The character was played by Gary Cooper in the film *High Noon*.

14. Igor Stravinsky. He believed that Bach was the most modern of composers.

15. The Land of Nod. Although he was actually sent wandering, Cain went there after he slew Abel.

16. Hialeah Race Track. Near Miami, the track installed the first camera in 1936.

17. "Stella Dallas." One of the original "soaps," this show was popular for many decades.

18. Rogers Hornsby. He batted .424 with the St. Louis Cardinals in 1924.

19. Macropodidae. Smaller members of the kangaroo family include some rabbit-sized wallabies.

20. Abbott Suger. Head of the Benedictine monastery, he was the guiding genius of Paris's Abbey of St. Denis, which unified all the elements of Gothic architecture.

21. "Notes from the Underground." The story was written by Dostoyevsky.

22. The New Christy Minstrels. She was in her teens at the time.

23. Dingo Bar. The meeting occurred in May, 1925, and commenced one of the great literary friendships of twentieth-century literature.

24. Pawnbroker. He was played by Rod Steiger in the film of the same name.

25. The lowest bone of the spine. It consists of five vertebrae.

26. Warren Beatty. In the TV series "The Many Loves of Dobie Gillis," he was the big man on campus who competed for the affections of Thalia Menninger (played by Tuesday Weld).

27. University of Michigan. Located in Ann Arbor, the stadium seats 101,701 fans.

28. Writing of the "Star Spangled Banner." Francis Scott Key was imprisoned on the ship when he composed our national anthem.

29. Cacambo. He was part Spanish and part Argentine and had been a chorister, verger, sailor, monk and commercial traveler.

30. Mt. Waialeale, Kauai, in Hawaii. It has an annual average rainfall of 460 inches.

YOUR MIGH-T.I.Q.

Since THE INQUISITION is tantamount to a final exam on all the categories in this book, it seems fitting that your scores on this particular chapter be equated to a super trivia intelligence quotient or Migh-T.I.Q. Take the number of correct answers from THE INQUISITION and see what kind of Migh-T.I.Q. you've acquired by the index below.

Number of Correct Answers	Rating
1–5	A VALIANT TRY
6–10	AN "A" FOR EFFORT
11–15	WHIZ KID
16–20	AHEAD OF THE PACK
21–25	MENTAL FAST LANE
26–30	MOVE OVER, EINSTEIN!

About the Author

Norm Chandler Fox co-authored *Violent Sundays* (Simon & Schuster, 1984), is a contributing editor to *Los Angeles* magazine, writes daytime television serials and primetime episodic television, and paints in his spare time. A graduate of Harvard College and the Graduate School of Business at Columbia University, he lives with his television executive-writer spouse, Loreen Arbus, and a fierce four-pound Yorkshire Terrier, Skoshi, in Hollywood, where they all collect trivia.